LENA
HORNE

LENA HORNE

Leslie Palmer

Senior Consulting Editor
Nathan Irvin Huggins
Director
W.E.B. Du Bois Institute for Afro-American Research
Harvard University

CHELSEA HOUSE PUBLISHERS
New York   Philadelphia

Chelsea House Publishers

Editor-in-Chief   Nancy Toff
Executive Editor   Remmel T. Nunn
Managing Editor   Karyn Gullen Browne
Copy Chief   Juliann Barbato
Picture Editor   Adrian G. Allen
Art Director   Maria Epes
Manufacturing Manager   Gerald Levine

Black Americans of Achievement

Senior Editor   Richard Rennert

Staff for LENA HORNE

Associate Editor   Perry King
Deputy Copy Chief   Ellen Scordato
Editorial Assistant   Jennifer Trachtenberg
Picture Researcher   Joan Kathryn Beard
Assistant Art Director   Laurie Jewell
Designer   Ghila Krajzman
Production Coordinator   Joseph Romano
Cover Illustration   Alan Nahajian

First Printing

1 3 5 7 9 8 6 4 2

Library of Congress Cataloging-in-Publication Data

Palmer, Leslie.
   Lena Horne / Leslie Palmer ; senior consulting editor, Nathan
Irvin Huggins.
      p.   cm.–(Black Americans of achievement)
   Bibliography: p
   Includes index.
   1. Horne, Lena.   2. Singers—United States—Biog-
raphy.   3. Afro-American singers—Biography.   I. Huggins,
Nathan Irvin, 1927–   .   II. Title. III. Series.
ML420.H65P3 1989   784.5′0092′4—dc19 [B]   88-30248
ISBN 1-55546-594-3   CIP
      0-7910-0226-8 (pbk.)   MN

CONTENTS

———— ❧ ————

BLACK AMERICANS OF ACHIEVEMENT

MUHAMMAD ALI
heavyweight champion

RICHARD ALLEN
founder of the
African Methodist
Episcopal church

LOUIS ARMSTRONG
musician

JAMES BALDWIN
author

BENJAMIN BANNEKER
scientist and
mathematician

MARY MCLEOD BETHUNE
educator

BLANCHE K. BRUCE
politician

RALPH BUNCHE
diplomat

GEORGE WASHINGTON CARVER
botanist

CHARLES WADDELL CHESTNUTT
author

PAUL CUFFE
abolitionist

FREDERICK DOUGLASS
abolitionist editor

CHARLES R. DREW
physician

W. E. B. DUBOIS
educator and author

PAUL LAURENCE DUNBAR
poet

DUKE ELLINGTON
bandleader and composer

RALPH ELLISON
author

ELLA FITZGERALD
singer

MARCUS GARVEY
black-nationalist leader

PRINCE HALL
social reformer

WILLIAM HASTIE
educator and politician

MATTHEW HENSON
explorer

CHESTER HIMES
author

BILLIE HOLIDAY
singer

JOHN HOPE
educator

LENA HORNE
entertainer

LANGSTON HUGHES
poet

JAMES WELDON JOHNSON
author

SCOTT JOPLIN
composer

MARTIN LUTHER KING, JR.
civil rights leader

JOE LOUIS
heavyweight champion

MALCOLM X
militant black leader

THURGOOD MARSHALL
Supreme Court justice

ELIJAH MUHAMMAD
religious leader

JESSE OWENS
champion athlete

GORDON PARKS
photographer

SIDNEY POITIER
actor

ADAM CLAYTON POWELL, JR.
political leader

A. PHILIP RANDOLPH
labor leader

PAUL ROBESON
singer and actor

JACKIE ROBINSON
baseball great

JOHN RUSSWURM
publisher

SOJOURNER TRUTH
antislavery activist

HARRIET TUBMAN
antislavery activist

NAT TURNER
slave revolt leader

DENMARK VESEY
slave revolt leader

MADAME C. J. WALKER
entrepreneur

BOOKER T. WASHINGTON
educator

WALTER WHITE
political activist

RICHARD WRIGHT
author

ON
ACHIEVEMENT

Coretta Scott King

BEFORE YOU BEGIN this book, I hope you will ask yourself what the word *excellence* means to you. I think that it's a question we should all ask and keep asking as we grow older and change. Because the truest answer to it should never change. When you think of excellence, perhaps you think of success at work; or of becoming wealthy; or meeting the right person, getting married, and having a good family life.

Those important goals are worth striving for, but there is a better way to look at excellence. As Martin Luther King, Jr., said in one of his last sermons, "I want you to be first in love. I want you to be first in moral excellence. I want you to be first in generosity. If you want to be important, wonderful. If you want to be great, wonderful. But recognize that he who is greatest among you shall be your servant."

My husband, Martin Luther King, Jr., knew that the true meaning of achievement is service. When I met him, in 1952, he was already ordained as a Baptist preacher and was working toward a doctoral degree at Boston University. I was studying at the New England Conservatory and dreamed of accomplishments in music. We married a year later, and after I graduated the following year we moved to Montgomery, Alabama. We didn't know it then, but our notions of achievement were about to undergo a dramatic change.

You may have read or heard about what happened next. What began with the boycott of a local bus line grew into a national movement, and by the time he was assassinated in 1968 my husband had fashioned a black movement powerful enough to shatter forever the practice of racial segregation. What you may not have read about is where he got his method for resisting injustice without compromising his religious beliefs.

He adopted the strategy of nonviolence from a man of a different race, who lived in a distant country, and even practiced a different religion. The man was Mahatma Gandhi, the great leader of India, who devoted his life to serving humanity in the spirit of love and nonviolence. It was in these principles that Martin discovered his method for social reform. More than anything else, those two principles were the key to his achievements.

This book is about black Americans who served society through the excellence of their achievements. It forms a part of the rich history of black men and women in America—a history of stunning accomplishments in every field of human endeavor, from literature and art to science, industry, education, diplomacy, athletics, jurisprudence, even polar exploration.

Not all of the people in this history had the same ideals, but I think you will find something that all of them have in common. Like Martin Luther King, Jr., they all decided to become "drum majors" and serve humanity. In that principle—whether it was expressed in books, inventions, or song—they found something outside themselves to use as a goal and a guide. Something that showed them a way to serve others, instead of living only for themselves.

Reading the stories of these courageous men and women not only helps us discover the principles that we will use to guide our own lives but also teaches us about our black heritage and about America itself. It is crucial for us to know the heroes and heroines of our history and to realize that the price we paid in our struggle for equality in America was dear. But we must also understand that we have gotten as far as we have partly because America's democratic system and ideals made it possible.

We are still struggling with racism and prejudice. But the great men and women in this series are a tribute to the spirit of our democratic ideals and the system in which they have flourished. And that makes their stories special and worth knowing. ◆

LENA
HORNE

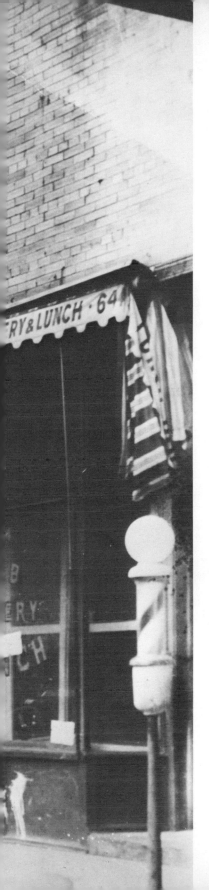

1

TALL, TAN,
AND
TERRIFIC!

ONE FALL MORNING in 1933, while her friends trooped off to high school, 16-year-old Lena Horne went instead to the Cotton Club. This fashionable cabaret, located in the uptown district of Harlem, stood at the center of New York City's glittery nighttime world. Every evening, a unique assortment of celebrities, socialites, and well-known mobsters motored to the northeast corner of Lenox Avenue and 142nd Street. There they passed through a modest doorway and entered the most exotic night spot in the city.

Artificial palm trees and wooden posts gave the interior of the Cotton Club a jungle look; expensive draperies and fixtures softened the primitive decor and added a sense of luxury. Amid this provocative setting, elegantly dressed men and women sat at tables and booths around a small wooden stage, drinking illicit alcohol (liberally supplied by the syndicate-backed management in violation of the 18th Amendment to the Constitution) and dining on everything from steak and lobster to Chinese food. The specialty of the house, however, was its hot entertainment.

From 1923 to 1936, this undistinguished building in New York's uptown district of Harlem housed the Cotton Club, the most exclusive cabaret in the city. Horne's first professional audition took place there in 1933, when she was 16 years old.

Twice each year, the Cotton Club served up a new and spectacular floor show featuring eye-popping costumes and elaborately staged routines. Every production was rapidly paced. As soon as one act departed from the limelight, another highly acclaimed group of performers paraded in from the wings.

To make the revues even more distinctive, the Cotton Club showcased only black entertainers. Management took this restriction one step further when selecting young women to star in its glamorous chorus line, which was the cabaret's top attraction. All of these dancers had to be light skinned.

Blacks may have commanded the stage at the Cotton Club, but they were virtually never admitted as customers. Only a few light-skinned blacks who could pass for white were permitted inside. It was a startling—although not unprecedented—policy of racial discrimination in a community with the largest black population in the country, and it added to the Cotton Club's tremendous mystique. According to Cab Calloway, leader of the house orchestra, "Ne-

The Cotton Club's lively floor shows featured exquisitely (and sometimes revealingly) costumed dancers in an intimate setting. All of the dance numbers—including this routine, which was part of Horne's very first revue, the "Stormy Weather Show"—had "a primitive naked quality that was supposed to make a civilized audience lose its inhibitions," Horne said.

groes from the Harlem community would line up out-side to watch the limousines drive up—Cadillacs and Rolls-Royces and Duesenbergs long enough to make you choke."

Like many Harlem residents, Horne logged a lot of hours tuning in to the twice-weekly live radio broadcasts of jazz and blues that issued from the Cotton Club. Swooning to the silvery sounds of Duke Ellington's "Mood Indigo" and Calloway's "Minnie the Moocher," she began to feel as though the stage where they performed was a familiar place. But on the fall morning that she approached the two-story building and climbed the long stairway that led to the top-floor cabaret, she was not at all relaxed. It was her first time inside the posh nightclub, and she had not come there as a customer.

Horne was looking to land a job—one of two openings in the chorus line—so she could help sup-port her mother and her stepfather, who were having a difficult time making ends meet. They were among the 100,000 Harlemites (nearly half of the district's total population) who depended on relief organiza-tions to help them check the ravaging effects of the Great Depression. Her mother, who accompanied her to the club, was responsible for arranging the audi-tion, the first in Lena's bid to become a professional dancer.

Edna Rodriguez knew her willowy daughter had talent as well as striking beauty, but she also knew firsthand the price most performers had to pay to become a success: a grueling life of travel from one town to the next. Lena's mother had spent many long and difficult years as an actress with several touring theater companies. When she began to transfer her own dreams of being a successful entertainer to her tall, graceful daughter, she made up her mind that Lena should start at the top: Owney Madden's Cotton Club.

Lena's mother called upon Elida Webb, an old friend and former acting colleague who was dance captain at the showplace. Webb thought that Lena was too young for a spot in the chorus line—most of the female dancers were close to 20 years old. Nevertheless, she arranged for the teenager to try out for an upcoming revue that, like all of the club's musical productions, would be staged as lavishly as possible.

The Cotton Club extravaganzas had been acknowledged as the height of New York entertainment ever since the stage curtains first parted in 1923. Bigtime gangster Owney Madden had opened the ballroom so it could serve as an outlet for Madden's No. 1 beer, an illicit brew that brought in huge, illegal profits. But it actually turned out to be the black dancers, singers, and musicians who drew the customers, and the club's jutting stage soon became known as a launching pad for a number of performers, especially bandleader and composer Duke Ellington, who used the venue to spread the gospel of jazz throughout the musical world.

Two of the top attractions at the Cotton Club during the 1930s were dancer Bill ("Bojangles") Robinson (left) and bandleader Cab Calloway (right). Harlem's leading cabaret, which featured only black performers but usually did not admit black patrons, was more than just a segregated night spot, according to Calloway. "It was a club," he said, "where you had to be somebody to get in there."

On the morning of Lena's audition, however, the Cotton Club held none of the glamour and excitement she had imagined it would. Instead of finding a cabaret brimming with music and laughter, she entered a dark, horseshoe-shaped room in which the air was heavy with stale cigarette smoke. Tiny tables and upended chairs took up almost every available space on the two-tiered floor. The club usually accommodated about 700 people at each show, but on this fateful morning, it was almost empty.

A work lamp cast a single spotlight on the small stage. Herman Stark, the gruff, cigar-chomping manager of the club, scrutinized each hopeful chorus girl as she was directed to stand in the light. At his signal, the rehearsal pianist began to play the accompaniment to a song-and-dance routine. Lena and her mother watched with Stark.

An audition can be an unnerving, even frightening, prospect for anyone, young or old, inexperienced or seasoned. The performer must try to project the very best of his or her abilities in front of a judge whose sole purpose is to weed out the talented entertainers from those with lesser gifts. Alone in the spotlight, the anxious performer has only a short time to distill all the hours of rehearsal into a single, sparkling presentation. Most auditions are over in minutes. But Stark was not even that patient. He interrupted each young woman after only a few seconds, saying, "That's enough."

As Lena watched the other performances, her heart pounded. "I could carry a tune," she later wrote in her autobiography (*Lena*, cowritten with Richard Schickel), "but I could hardly have been called a singer; I could . . . dance a little, but I could hardly be called a dancer. I was tall and skinny and I had very little going for me except a pretty face and long, long hair that framed it rather nicely."

A stagestruck teenager, Horne left secretarial school in the fall of 1933 to garner one of two openings in the chorus line of the Cotton Club. She is shown here the following summer, when she was winding up her first year at the cabaret.

Horne (fourth from right) in a 1934 performance at the Cotton Club. The elite of white society flocked there to see what management called "the cream of sepia talent . . . a chorus of bronze beauties."

Lena tried to compose herself when Stark called her name. She stepped slowly toward the stage and positioned herself in the tiny area lit by the work lamp. While waiting for the piano accompaniment to begin, she peered into the hazy surroundings but was unable to make out the face of her mother or any other member of the small, watchful audience.

Suddenly, Lena noticed that the pianist had already started to play, and then she realized in horror that she could not move her feet. The dance steps she had spent hours practicing and perfecting would not come to her. All was lost.

Then Lena heard her mother's voice urging her on, and her stage fright subsided. She began to sing and dance, and the sheer sensation of movement—spinning and whirling as fast as she could—removed her last traces of self-doubt. When the music came to an end, she was still dancing furiously, lost in the joy of performance. Everyone in the room, including the surly manager of the club, broke instantly into loud applause. She was hired.

Lena appeared in three shows each night—at 8:30 and 11:30 P.M. and at 2:00 A.M.—and also performed with the chorus line at local vaudeville houses and business conventions. All of these appearances netted her a total of $25 per week—far more than secretaries or salesclerks could hope to make. In fact, it was such a good salary for depression-ridden America that she had no choice but to stop attending high school.

As soon as the school authorities realized that Lena had quit Wadleigh High, they dispatched a truant officer to call on her family. Every week, her mother's response to the officer's questions regarding Lena's whereabouts was the same: "Missing." The officer eventually found out why the wayward schoolgirl was never in class, but, according to Lena, he "could not bring himself to force me to return to school, knowing that I was the principal support of that household." Instead of going back to the classroom, she remained in the dazzling world of show business as a scantily dressed member of the Cotton Club's chorus line. Management billed the ensemble as the most beautiful "tall, tan, and terrific" show girls in America.

To her mother, such a billing was the pinnacle of success. But for Lena Horne, it was only the beginning. 〰

2
STORMY WEATHER

LENA MARY CALHOUN Horne was born on June 30, 1917, in Brooklyn, New York, and was immediately perceived as different from other blacks. At the small Jewish hospital where she was delivered, the nursing staff mistook her mother for a white woman after seeing her extremely light complexion and thus expected the newborn's skin to be white as well. When Lena's skin turned out to be a beautiful copper hue instead, the nurses made a tremendous fuss over the baby. They took turns carrying her up and down the halls of the maternity ward, showing her off to equally surprised onlookers.

Lena had inherited her distinctive color and radiant good looks from her father, Teddy, who was not at the hospital because he was taking part in a card game. A devoted gambler, he was trying to win enough money to cover the cost of his wife and daughter's hospital bills. He was, according to Lena, "a man of the street—a renegade," and very much the black sheep of the Horne clan, one of Brooklyn's leading black families.

Headed by Lena's grandparents Edwin and Cora—southerners who first arrived in New York City in 1896—the Hornes belonged to a tightly knit, middle-class community known as the black bourgeoisie. Established shortly after the Civil War ended in 1865, this elite group was originally made up of blacks who felt extremely privileged because they were lucky

Edna Scottron Horne holds her newborn daughter, Lena, in 1917. The child was raised by her grandparents in Brooklyn after being abandoned by her parents.

The Freeman, *a national black newspaper, features Lena's grandfather Edwin Horne in an article recommending him for political office. An extremely well-respected member of the black bourgeoisie, he was actually a mulatto (he was born in Tennessee to a white father and Native American mother) whose parents thought he would face less discrimination if he classed himself as a black rather than an Indian.*

enough not to have been field hands in the days of slavery. They resided primarily in Boston, New York, Philadelphia, and Washington, D.C., where they formed a mutually supportive network and enjoyed a life very different from that of most other blacks.

In post–Civil War America, white society denied the majority of blacks decent jobs, good housing, and a solid education. The black bourgeoisie nonetheless managed to create a self-contained world in which its inhabitants rarely suffered from the racial injustices fostered by Jim Crow laws—laws that called for separate, and invariably unequal, public facilities for blacks and whites. It was a world that reflected the beliefs and values held by white middle-class Americans and that also enabled blacks to experience many of the comforts enjoyed by their white counterparts.

Lena was, as she later wrote in her autobiography, "a stranger in the world which most Negroes inhabit and with which they are forced, from birth, to come to terms." The Brooklyn community into which she was born had its own debutante balls, literary societies, and fraternities. Her family, she said, was "isolated from the mainstream of Negro life, seeing a relatively narrow group of people."

Among the most valued undertakings of families such as the Hornes was the pursuit of higher learning. A good education was considered by the black middle class to be an essential ingredient for those who wanted to lead a rich and meaningful life. In fact, most of the nation's blacks who received advanced degrees in the first half of the 20th century were descendants of the approximately 500 families who initially composed the black bourgeoisie.

Yet life in well-to-do black strongholds such as Brooklyn was far from perfect. Even though the cultural and educational opportunities for middle-class blacks far exceeded what was available to other black Americans, they could aspire only to certain professions, especially teaching, medicine, shopkeeping, and the clergy, in which they served other blacks. Lucrative white-collar jobs, for the most part, were controlled by whites and remained closed to blacks.

Horne spent much of her youth in the heart of New York's black middle class, closely watched by her grandparents Edwin and Cora Horne. They lived in a narrow, four-story brownstone surrounded by a black iron fence, with a large garden in the rear.

Lena's mother, Edna (above), and father, Teddy (opposite), came from well-regarded families in Brooklyn and seemed to be a perfect match for one another. Their marriage did not last for very long, however.

Lena's father never took to the middle-class values revered by his kin. His marriage to Edna Scottron, the attractive and somewhat pampered daughter of a prominent Brooklyn family, was seemingly a match made in heaven, and they lived on the top floor of his parents' comfortable four-story brownstone at 189 Chauncey Street. Yet Teddy, who held an excellent position with the New York State Department of Labor at the time of Lena's birth, was much more interested in making money, preferably without doing too much work, than in being respectable.

By the time Lena was three years old, her father had decided the working world was definitely not for him. He started to frequent gambling spots in Harlem, where easy money could be made, and, according to Lena, " 'the other world' got him for good." Late in 1920, he abandoned his wife and child and headed west in search of bigger and better, though most likely illegal, opportunities. On occasion, he sent money to help them out.

Without Teddy to look after her, Lena's mother was miserable. An extremely genteel woman, she did not get along with her estranged husband's parents, especially Lena's stern and domineering grandmother, and found it hard to accept the failure of a marriage that had begun so promisingly. She longed to escape from her unhappy life and began to dream about becoming a famous actress.

A short time after her husband left the household, Edna decided to run away from Brooklyn and seek out her dreams. She joined the Lafayette Players, a black stock company founded in 1914 to promote serious drama and associated with Harlem's distinguished Lafayette Theatre, where actors Charles Gilpin and Paul Robeson were headliners. In doing so, she deserted her daughter, leaving Lena to live with her grandparents and her uncle Burke, the youngest of Teddy's three brothers.

For the next four years, Lena was raised in a peculiar household. Her grandparents, often at odds with each other, slept in separate rooms and hardly talked to one another. Yet their strong and distinct personalities helped shape her character.

Edwin Horne, at various stages in his life a poet, teacher, journalist, publisher, and politician, was a highly cultured man. He spoke six languages and was deeply interested in the arts. He often took Lena to the theater, the ballet, museums, and other cultural spots in New York City. At home, he played his large collection of records for her and told her about America's great black entertainers, among them singer Florence Mills and Shakespearean actor Ira Aldrich.

Whereas her grandfather schooled Lena in the arts, her grandmother taught Lena to be civic-minded, particularly in matters of race. The former Cora Calhoun had a tremendous social conscience and worked tirelessly for the National Association for the Advancement of Colored People (NAACP) and the National Urban League, two of the nation's leading antidiscriminatory organizations. She also fought for women to be given the right to vote and helped found the National Association of Colored Women, another activist group.

Even before Lena started to attend school, she accompanied her grandmother to meetings of the NAACP and other organizations. "I was always the only child there," she said in her autobiography, "sitting quietly, listening because I knew I would be questioned later about what I had heard." During one of these visits, she became, at the age of two, a cover girl for the October 1919 issue of the NAACP's *Branch Bulletin*. The cover shows Lena, in a white hat and dress, clutching a rose, with an unhappy expression on her face.

Lena was thus shepherded by her grandparents, especially her grandmother, during the early years of

Horne, at the age of two, poses for a cover of the National Association for the Advancement of Colored People's Branch Bulletin. By the time this photograph was taken for the October 1919 issue, Lena's grandmother had already enrolled her as a member of this influential antidiscrimination organization.

her life. As a result, she seldom enjoyed the companionship of people her own age. "My association with children," she said later, "was limited to just a few in the neighborhood who met with Grandmother's approval."

Lena was not the only child to fall under the watchful eye of the diminutive Cora Horne, whose habit of lecturing other youngsters in the neighborhood won her the nickname of the "Tiny Terror." The sight of this fiery woman scolding the boys who hung around street corners instead of going to school was a familiar one to many youths in New York City. The most notable among them was Paul Robeson, a longtime friend of the family who obtained a scholarship to Rutgers University with Cora's help and later embarked on a remarkable singing and acting career.

When Lena was old enough to attend kindergarten, her grandmother established a scholarship at the Ethical Culture School near Fort Greene Park in Brooklyn, and Lena became the first recipient of Cora's endowment. Every day, her uncle Burke escorted her to the private school and brought her home as soon as the final bell rang: Cora heartily disapproved of Lena remaining after school to play with her friends. "My grandmother," Lena said, "did not believe in idle chitchat for herself or for anyone else."

Although Lena was carefully nurtured by her grandparents, sympathetic neighbors called her Salvation Sal. It was a nickname that resulted from the breakup of her parents' marriage and had much to do with the prevailing view of divorce. In the 1920s, divorce was very rare, and the dissolution of her parents' marriage was considered quite scandalous.

The breakup certainly troubled Lena. Every night, she said her prayers and then kissed the photographs of her mother and father that she kept in her bedroom. Occasionally, she received gifts from them: clothes and toys.

Lena's grandparents kept her posted as to her father's whereabouts, but they never mentioned Edna, whom Lena nevertheless saw briefly on a few occasions. As a member of the Lafayette Players, Edna managed to nab leading roles in several theater productions featuring the group, including *The Count of Monte Cristo* and *Dr. Jekyll and Mr. Hyde.* Her cousins, without telling Cora, brought Lena to two of these performances. During the first of these visits, Lena made her stage debut, appearing in a scene in *Madame X.*

Aside from these few shining moments, Edna's stage career never really flourished. Employment for any actress has always been intermittent at best, and it was especially difficult in the 1920s for a black performer to find many acting opportunities. Lena's mother struggled to find steady work and failed to

Cora Horne (seated, center) established herself as a prominent civic leader while directing a unit of the American Red Cross. Her affiliation with this and a number of other important organizations—including the National Urban League, the National Council of Women, and Big Sisters—helped spark her granddaughter Lena's interest in public service.

One of the first showplaces in Harlem to admit black patrons, the Lafayette Theatre housed an important drama company: the all-black Lafayette Players, established by the noted actor Charles Gilpin. Lena's mother was a member of this unique group, which performed legitimate theater—serious dramas and revivals of hit Broadway shows—instead of the usual fare for black entertainers: comedy acts and vaudeville routines.

become a major star of the stage. Nevertheless, she starred in real-life melodramas of her own making.

One sunny day in 1924, when Lena was alone in the house, her cousin Augusta Byrd came to the door and announced to the seven year old that her mother was very sick and needed to see her. They took a cab to a Harlem apartment, where Lena's mother lay bedridden. After the two hugged and kissed, Lena was told by her mother that they would be together from then on. "She said," according to Lena, "she had to get me away from my grandmother's because she knew my father was going to kidnap me from there."

Teddy had no intention of kidnapping his daughter; he was quite happy for Lena to remain at Chaun-

cey Street while he sent money to support her. It was
Edna who had elected to change her daughter's living
arrangements by resorting to subterfuge. She had decided that Cora was a terrible influence on Lena (Edna
had conveniently forgotten that she had deserted her
daughter in the first place).

Lena was excited by the prospect of living with
her mother again. Edna was not only "so beautiful,"
she said, but, unlike the child's reserved grandparents, she was also happy to shower Lena with affec-
tion. Brooklyn may have been Lena's home, but she
was not at all disappointed to leave it.

Lena and her mother stayed in Philadelphia for
a month, then boarded a Pullman sleeper and headed
south to Miami, Florida, where Edna had lined up
several acting jobs. When their train pulled into
Washington, D.C., before pushing on into the Deep
South, Lena and her mother were informed by railroad personnel that they were occupying whites-only
accommodations and that they must leave the sleeper.
According to Jim Crow laws, blacks were not allowed
to ride in any segregated cars reserved for whites.

For the rest of the long journey, Lena and her
mother were forced to sit in an uncomfortable coach
at the front of the train, right behind the noisy en-
gine. This was Lena's rude introduction to legally
enforced racial segregation. For the first time in her
life, she experienced what most of the blacks in the
United States—those who did not live in a self-
contained world—had to put up with every day of
their life. Other encounters with racial prejudice soon
followed.

In Miami, Lena and her mother moved into a
small frame house that belonged to a former acting
colleague of Edna's, Lucille Noble. Lena was enrolled
in a one-room school, where a single teacher was in
charge of five grades. It was a world apart from the
private school she had attended in Brooklyn, and she

Horne at around the age of 12, outside her mother's and Lucille Noble's home in Miami, Florida. Lena later said of her stay there, "I was obsessed with the idea that I had to be good, that my mother must never hear anything bad about me."

was allowed to skip a grade. But she did not find everything at this school to be so easy. The students made fun of her fair skin and mimicked her northern accent.

Lena adapted by acting. "I learned to change my accent," she said, ". . . and I learned to play politics so I wouldn't get thrown in the dirt and be punished when I got home for ruining my clothes. Most important of all, I learned to bury Lena Calhoun Horne, my grandmother's little lady, in a corner of my brain. She was no use to me now."

After only a few months in Miami, Edna pulled up her stakes again, this time taking Lena to another Florida city, Jacksonville. Other moves followed—such were the demands of Edna's life as an actress. Sometimes, Lena went with her mother. But most of the time Lena was left with strangers while her mother, still stagestruck, pursued her dreams of stardom. "Until I was in my early teens," Lena said, "I was never to spend more than a few months with my mother at any single time."

Not long after the pair arrived in Jacksonville, Edna and several of her friends decided to see the Silas Green Tent Show, a black vaudeville revue playing outside of town, and they asked Lena to join them. It was not often that she was invited on such excursions. The group piled into a car, their spirits high in anticipation of a fun-filled evening.

Just as the car neared the tent show, a black man along the road flagged them down. He told them to drive out of the area as fast as they could because there was going to be a lynching. Lena barely understood what was happening, yet she felt tremendous fear surge through each adult as their car raced home through the dark, forbidding night.

Shortly after this incident, Lena was sent back to her grandparents' house in Brooklyn. Her visit was happy but brief. She spent the next three years shuttling back and forth between Brooklyn, where she attended Public School 70, and wherever her mother could find employment. Lena quickly learned not to become too attached to people. "I never let myself love anybody," Lena maintained, "because I knew I couldn't stay around."

In 1927, Lena's mother contacted Frank Horne, the only member of the Horne family with whom she had remained friendly, and asked him to take care of Lena for a while. He agreed, and once again Lena moved to a new home, this one in Fort Valley, Georgia.

Frank was the second youngest of Edwin and Cora's four sons, and he was the reigning intellectual of the Horne family. This became clear in 1925, when his

Horne developed a penchant for performing when she realized that she had to act like her fellow students in the South if she wanted to get along with them. Lena is shown here (center) in 1927, embracing two of her classmates in Miami.

poetry was anthologized in Alain Locke's *The New Negro*, a collection of stories and verse that signaled the beginning of the Harlem Renaissance, a period of black artistic and cultural enlightenment that revolved around New York's uptown district. That same year, he won an honorable mention in a literary contest sponsored by the National Urban League's *Opportunity* magazine to determine the best black writers in America (the prizewinners were the poets Countee Cullen and Langston Hughes).

Frank was a man of many talents. Although trained as an eye doctor, he was a professor of English, dean of students, and assistant to the president at Fort Valley Junior Industrial College when Lena came to stay with him in 1927. She lived in the girls' dormitory with his fiancée, Frankye Bunn, and then, when her uncle and Frankye were married in 1928, she moved into their house. She attended a local school, the Rosenwald Endowed Public Grade School, and once again felt compelled to change her northern accent so her schoolmates would not treat her harshly.

During her stay at Fort Valley, Lena did not always have to pretend to be uncultured. Around her

In 1927, Horne moved with her mother to Macon, Georgia, and then to nearby Fort Valley to live with her uncle Frank. She stayed in a girls' dormitory on the campus of Fort Valley Junior Industrial College before joining her uncle and his wife in this house the following year.

uncle and his educated circle of friends, she felt free to be her true, urbane self. She especially delighted in the intelligent, sparkling conversation of these adults.

On a warm spring day in 1928, an extremely handsome man—more sophisticated than anyone Lena had ever met—showed up in Fort Valley, driving an expensive automobile. It was her father. Lena barely remembered him, except from photographs. But she was dazzled by Teddy Horne nonetheless. Independent and outspoken, he was full of advice for his young daughter, always reminding her to be strong in character. He stayed for about a month and then traveled back to his sporting life in Pittsburgh, Pennsylvania, where he had settled down with his second wife, Irene, and ran a small hotel.

Lena's happy stay in Fort Valley ended abruptly in 1929, when her mother came to retrieve her once again. They headed to Atlanta, Georgia, where Edna and Lucille Noble had bought a house. Soon, the two actresses had to go on the road again, and Edna left her daughter with a housekeeper whom Lena called Aunt May. Every day after Lena attended Booker T. Washington Junior High School, she returned home to do household chores. Once she completed her tasks, Aunt May donned white gloves and ran her hands over the places that Lena was to have cleaned. If any dirt showed up on the gloves, Aunt May made a mental note of it. Then, on Wednesday and Saturday evenings, Aunt May punished Lena for her oversights: She beat the 12 year old with a wooden switch.

Lena never complained to her mother about the beatings. But neighbors who had heard Lena's screams of pain eventually told Edna about the lashings. The housekeeper was immediately dismissed, and a short time later, Lena was sent back north to her grandparents' house in Brooklyn. Her mother, according

Visits with her uncle Frank and his wife, Frankye, greatly stimulated Lena's intellectual life. No matter whether they were based in Fort Valley, Georgia, or in Washington, D.C., her aunt and uncle were usually surrounded by a coterie of highly educated and well-regarded people—including singer-actor Paul Robeson and Walter White, the executive secretary of the National Association for the Advancement of Colored People—and made it a practice to introduce them to Lena.

to Lena, "finally accepted the fact that her attempts to take sole responsibility for me were doomed to failure."

Back on Chauncey Street, Lena did not have to change her accent or worry about the color of her skin. She was again a member of Brooklyn's black elite. Slowly but surely, she began to remove the defenses she had erected during her years in the South. She stopped feeling put upon and powerless.

Horne generally felt much more secure in her old neighborhood in Brooklyn than in the Deep South, where she often tried to deny her middle-class origins. She is shown here at the age of 12, wearing a fur coat that was a gift from her father.

Lena resumed her education by attending Public School 35 and then, in September 1929, enrolled in Brooklyn's ornate Girls High School. She joined the Peter Pan Club, a social club for young girls, and later graduated to another privileged society, the Junior Debs. She was also encouraged to participate in dramatics and dancing by Laura Rollock, an old family friend with whom she stayed while her grandmother went abroad that autumn on a trip financed by Teddy's gambling successes.

It was an exciting time for Lena. Laura Rollock, like Cora Horne, was active in the National Urban League and the NAACP. But unlike Cora, she thought it was good for Lena to socialize and thus sent her to the Anna Jones Dancing School. Lena was well prepared for the experience: She had taken dancing les-

Horne's life took a pleasant turn in the fall of 1929, when her grandmother embarked on an extended tour of Europe. Lena, who had enrolled that September in Girls High School in Brooklyn (shown here), was free to join her childhood friends at clubs and social gatherings that had been off limits to her in the South and under her grandmother's stewardship.

Horne (front row, far right) with some of her friends in the Junior Debs, a social club for young women. As a teenager, Lena took acting and singing lessons and often displayed her theatrical talents at Junior Deb tea parties.

sons, at her mother's insistence, during her forays in the South.

While attending the Anna Jones Dancing School, Lena got her first taste of what it was like to perform on a big stage. Her class won an opportunity to dance at the Harlem Opera House, one of New York's handsomest theaters. Their performance was accompanied by "Stormy Weather," a romantic tune that soon became a hit after it was popularized by vocalist Ethel Waters at the Cotton Club revue.

As Lena plunged into Brooklyn's social world, she discovered her own theatrical talents. She landed the lead role in the annual charity show put on by the Junior Theatre Guild of Brooklyn and, though only a teenager, brought down the house with her sweet voice and marvelous stage presence. It began to seem to her that the performing arts might have a place in her future.

But before Lena could make any definite plans, her life became unsettled once again. In September 1932, her grandmother died of bronchial asthma, and her grandfather passed away several months later. Because her uncle Burke was far too young to take care of her, Lena moved out of her Chauncey Street home and went to live once more with Laura Rollock.

Then Lena's errant mother surfaced again, this time with her new husband, Miguel ("Mike") Rodriguez, whom she had met while she was performing in Cuba. In 1933, the newlyweds decided to move to Brooklyn and wrote to Lena that they wanted her to live with them. Lena was crushed by their request. She was happy where she was and did not want to repeat the past miseries of living with her mother. She had seen enough of Edna's unreliable ways.

Furthermore, Lena was still smarting from what had taken place immediately after her grandmother died. Edna ordered her daughter to stay away from Cora's funeral, but Lena refused to listen. She stormed out of the brownstone, with her mother right on her heels. Edna finally caught up with her daughter just as she reached the front door of the funeral parlor, and she dragged Lena home—to the astonishment of the rest of the family.

Despite this incident, Lena agreed to join her mother and stepfather. They started off by sharing a Brooklyn apartment. Their black neighbors, however, were not very accepting of the fact that Lena's mother had married a white man, and they treated

Mrs. Horne, Civic Leader, Succumbs

Funeral Held for Woman Who Served in Numerous Movements in City and Nation—Rites Private

Leader Dies

Mrs. Cora Horne.

In September 1932, the Brooklyn Eagle *printed this obituary notice about Cora Horne. The newspaper described Lena's grandmother as "prominent over a period of 27 years in the civic and social world of Brooklyn" and listed many of the widely known organizations of which she was a member.*

Lena at the age of 15, shortly before she moved into an apartment close to Chauncey Street with her mother and stepfather. Within a year's time, the threesome left Brooklyn for another New York City borough, the Bronx, and then moved again, to Harlem in Manhattan.

the family quite rudely. Such resentment was, Lena said, her "first introduction to the prejudice of the Negro against the white. It can be as intense as its reverse."

In 1933, the family moved to a small apartment in another New York City borough, the Bronx. Lena was forced to leave her old friends behind as she entered Wadleigh Night High School, a secretarial school. No longer in a middle-class neighborhood, she made few friends.

Mike encountered some difficulties as well. In his new neighborhood, he had a hard time finding steady employment. Although he was eager to work, his command of the English language was very poor and limited his ability to land a decent job. The Great Depression, a time of scarce work opportunities, made finding a job even tougher for him. On top of these problems, he had a ferocious temper that was often triggered by his own misery at not being able to support his family. There was a great deal of tension in the small household, and it soon got worse.

Needing a cheaper place to live, the family moved again, this time to a tenement in Harlem. Their circumstances eventually became so dire that they had to rely on relief organizations for their groceries. More and more, it seemed to Lena that the answer to her family's problems—and her own, for she was very unhappy at Wadleigh Night High School in the Bronx—was for her to find work.

When her mother arranged an audition for her at the Cotton Club in the fall of 1933, Lena instantly agreed to try out for the job. She figured she had little to lose. However, she had no idea how much she was about to gain. ❦

3

PRESENTING
HELENA HORNE

———— ❧ ————

The COTTON CLUB was perhaps the most exclusive cabaret in Harlem when Lena began performing there in 1933, but the conditions for its employees were terrible. She was forced to share a tiny, cramped dressing room with the other chorus girls. They were discouraged from using the lone ladies' room in the night spot because the owners reserved it for the use of the paying customers. The kitchen was closed to the entertainers as well. Although the club's food, especially the Mexican dishes served during the first two shows and the fried chicken offered during the 2:00 A.M. performance, was reputed to be delicious, no member of the all-black cast was allowed to taste it.

When the Cotton Club first opened, members of the performers' families were not allowed to see any of the shows. They were admitted to the club only for final dress rehearsals. Even during these previews, they were not permitted to sit in the central part of the cabaret. They had to watch the shows from booths by the kitchen.

Strict adherence to the whites-only policy had become somewhat relaxed, however, by the time Lena began to work as a Cotton Club chorus girl. An elite group of blacks, mostly gamblers and underworld figures on close terms with the white gangsters who ran the place, often gained entrance to the otherwise-segregated ballroom. Nevertheless, they, too, had to sit in the side booths near the kitchen.

Horne performs "As Long as I Live" with Avon Long at the Cotton Club in 1934. The duet was her first featured role as a professional entertainer.

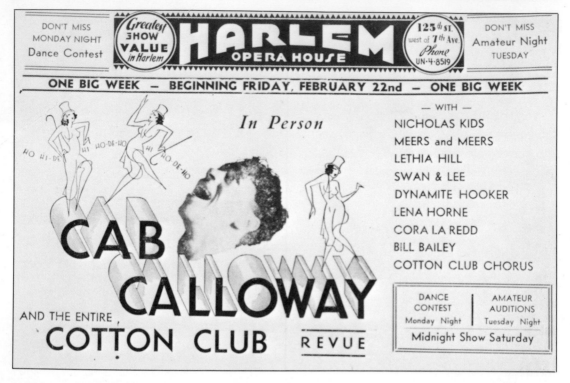

DON'T MISS
MONDAY NIGHT
Dance Contest

Greatest **SHOW** VALUE *in Harlem*

HARLEM
OPERA HOUSE

125th St.
west of 7th Ave
Phone
UN·4·8519

DON'T MISS
Amateur Night
TUESDAY

ONE BIG WEEK — BEGINNING FRIDAY, FEBRUARY 22nd — ONE BIG WEEK

HO HI-DE HI   HO-DE-HO   HI   HO DE-HO

In Person

— WITH —
NICHOLAS KIDS
MEERS and MEERS
LETHIA HILL
SWAN & LEE
DYNAMITE HOOKER
LENA HORNE
CORA LA REDD
BILL BAILEY
COTTON CLUB CHORUS

CAB CALLOWAY
AND THE ENTIRE
COTTON CLUB REVUE

DANCE CONTEST Monday Night	AMATEUR AUDITIONS Tuesday Night
Midnight Show Saturday	

Bandleader Cab Calloway is featured on a handbill announcing a week-long engagement of the Cotton Club revue at the Harlem Opera House in February 1935. Horne, whose name is listed on the flyer, had made her first appearance ever on a big stage almost five years before, at this very same theater.

When Teddy Horne was in town, he was among the privileged few to gain admittance to the club. He took pride in his talented daughter, who was the youngest member of the Cotton Club's renowned chorus line, and he and his friends went out of their way to protect the 16 year old from unwanted admirers. Lena, in turn, was expected to tell them if anyone was bothering her.

Not everything went smoothly for Lena as she began this new stage in her life. As had happened so often in the past, she found herself caught between two worlds. Members of the black middle class were not pleased with her. In their eyes, respectable young ladies did not become chorus girls in Harlem night spots. "My going to work in the club," she said in her autobiography, "caused quite a stir in the Negro press, to which my grandmother and her good works were well known."

Lena shrugged off their criticism just as she ignored the dreadful working conditions and the Cotton Club's questionable reputation. She was, she said, "still enough of a stage-struck kid to take some pride and pleasure in associating with the great talents who played the club." Floor show producer Lew Leslie and the highly prized songwriting team of Dorothy Fields and Jimmy McHugh had already left the Cotton Club by the time Lena started working there in 1933, but the club still showcased the top stars of the day. Among them were singers Adelaide Hall and Aida Ward, dancer Avon Long, actor Juano Hernandez, and the big bands of Claude Hopkins, Jimmy Lunceford, and, above all, Cab Calloway, who had replaced Duke Ellington as leader of the Cotton Club Orchestra in 1931.

Calloway befriended Lena shortly after he spotted her during her very first day of rehearsal. "My God," he exclaimed, "if it isn't the little squirt from Brooklyn!" They had originally met during Lena's days as a Junior Deb, when she had been a hostess at a charity affair featuring Calloway's band. Their second encounter marked the start of a fast friendship. He became an adviser and confidant to the woman he always called "Brooklyn."

Lena received less welcome attention from another adviser: her mother. Wanting to make sure that her daughter behaved in a manner befitting a future star, Edna accompanied Lena to work every night—much to the displeasure of the other chorus girls, who saw little need for another person to hang around in the already crowded backstage area. Under Edna's strict rules of conduct, Lena was forbidden to make friends with the older girls in the chorus line. "Actually, there was nothing to worry about," she said. "My very youth protected me."

Edna became, in effect, the classic stage mother. Her ambitions for her child overwhelmed all other

Lena with Joe Louis at his training camp in New Jersey several years after the sports-minded Teddy Horne introduced his teenage daughter to the boxing champ. Like many black Americans, she became a great admirer of Louis's, "who stood up to the white man," she said, "and beat him down with his fists."

considerations and made Lena an outcast among the club's closely knit community of performers. She was embraced by the club's management, however, because audiences appreciated her beauty and talent.

One night in the spring of 1934, during Lena's second revue at the Cotton Club, stage manager Herman Stark asked her to appear in her first featured role: a song-and-dance duet with Avon Long. Their act was performed to a Harold Arlen tune, "As Long as I Live." The audiences loved it and made it very clear that Lena had the makings of a leading lady.

The following fall, Lena was discovered by producer Lawrence Schwab, who had noticed her in the Cotton Club chorus line and decided she was perfect for a small role in his new musical, *Dance with Your Gods*. His offer excited Lena, but she was not permitted by the Cotton Club owners to join the show because she had been signed to an exclusive lifetime contract with the club. Anxious to see her daughter appear onstage, Edna had agreed with the club's management to a contract that prevented Lena from performing anywhere else.

Schwab would not be denied. He managed to get gangster Jack ("Legs") Diamond to intercede for him, and an agreement was reached with the Cotton Club management whereby Lena was allowed to skip the first show there each night to perform in the Broadway musical. After each performance of *Dance with Your Gods*, she quickly peeled off her costume, stepped into her Cotton Club outfit, and dashed to the subway, which deposited her uptown in time for the final two shows at the Harlem cabaret. Her schedule was so tight that she was never able to take her Broadway curtain call.

Teddy Horne attended Lena's Broadway debut. He was in town to see the 1934 Colored World Series Classic. The ball games, featuring black baseball players—all banned from the then-racially segregated major leagues—were held at nearby Yankee Stadium in the Bronx. At the end of each game, he made his way to the Broadway theater, where his daughter was billed last on the program and was required to do little more than an antic dance in an elaborately staged voodoo ceremony. The critics panned the show, and *Dance with Your Gods* closed after only a few performances.

Even though Lena's first Broadway musical flopped, Edna was convinced that stardom awaited her daughter. Both she and her husband started pressing the management of the Cotton Club to feature Lena in demanding solos and specialty acts. Lena's stepfather, Mike, even went so far as to threaten the management of the club, telling them Lena was going to quit unless she was given better spots in the shows. For his efforts, he was roughed up by some of Madden's men. All Lena got was a raise of five dollars per week.

After this violent encounter, Lena and her family decided that she had better leave the Cotton Club. Its owners clearly did not value her career. Yet they would not rescind their agreement, even though their lifetime contract with Lena—as well as with many of the other performers—was of questionable legality. The club's management knew that its employees would not contest their contracts because they could not foot the legal fees.

Lena had only one option if she wanted to break her contract with the Cotton Club: She had to run away. In 1935, she secured an audition in Philadelphia with bandleader Noble Sissle, who was looking for a female singer for his New York–based Society Orchestra. He had established his show-business reputation in 1921 when he teamed up with pianist Eubie Blake to write *Shuffle Along*, one of the first all-black musicals staged in a Broadway theater.

Unlike the Cotton Club band, Noble Sissle's Society Orchestra shied away from energetic jazz. It favored music pitched to the tastes of middle-class

Horne's stepfather, Miguel ("Mike") Rodriguez, was a former Cuban army officer who was known to take a combative stance in looking after Lena's career interests. She quickly decided to quit the Cotton Club after the racketeers who ran the cabaret roughed him up during one of their "business discussions."

audiences. For her audition, Lena sang just one number: an arrangement of "Dinner for One, Please, James." The tune, as it turned out, was a perfect choice for the proper, dignified style of singing that Sissle required. She was hired immediately.

Lena was a bit mystified by Sissle's enthusiasm for her. She later maintained, "When I think that really great singers like Ella Fitzgerald were singing with competing bands like Chick Webb's I don't see why Noble wanted me. I couldn't sing jazz and I couldn't sing blues. All I could do was carry a simple tune simply." But Sissle knew exactly what he was doing. He saw great potential in young Lena Horne and knew that all she needed was some coaching to improve her diction and phrasing.

Sissle became Lena's mentor. He also rechristened his young protégée so that her professional name would reflect the romance and style she projected onstage. He called her Helena Horne.

Performing with Sissle helped Lena refine her skills as both an actress and a singer. When the Society Orchestra played in cabarets and theaters, she was featured in a revue-type format: Her musical numbers were presented as self-contained sketches. She and Sissle sang a duet to open the show, using telephones as props; she was spotlighted on one side of the stage and he on the other side as they portrayed young lovers making a late-night romantic phone call. Singing "Dinner for One, Please, James," she was led to a seat at a table by singer Billy Banks, who was dressed as a waiter. Because Lena had not yet learned how to project her voice, a microphone was concealed in a flowerpot that sat on the table.

When the Society Orchestra played at dances, it presented a simple program—just music, no sketches. This format forced Lena to sharpen her skills as a vocalist. She sang mostly contemporary ballads, including "I Want to Be Kissed" and "Blue Moon."

When they were not singing, she and Billy Banks sat quietly in front of the orchestra, clad in short red jackets like the other band members.

Lena had gotten her first taste of life on the road while living with Edna as she pursued an acting career. As a member of the Noble Sissle Society Orchestra, Lena was on the road all of the time. Touring, she quickly discovered, can be a hard life for any performer. There are long bus rides, lodgings in dreary hotels, and bad meals.

For blacks, touring was even more difficult because of Jim Crow laws. Most hotel managers kept their places racially segregated and refused to rent rooms to blacks. As a result, Sissle's band usually had to locate a rooming house or a cheap hotel in the town's black section.

Singer Ella Fitzgerald was one of the chief practitioners of swing, a lively new form of jazz that swept the entire nation during the mid-1930s. Horne greatly admired her 17-year-old peer, who joined the Chick Webb Orchestra in 1935, at about the same time that Lena became the female vocalist with Noble Sissle's Society Orchestra.

These were not the only hardships that Lena had to face while on tour. Her mother and stepfather traveled with the band as her chaperons. "I felt exposed," Lena said of their presence. "I felt as if the whole world was being made privy to the secrets of my family's emotional life, the problems we had together."

Edna and Mike were not content to remain in the background. Just as they had done during Lena's Cotton Club days, they confronted her employer. Their most heated exchange with Sissle took place in 1936, when the Society Orchestra became the first black band invited to play at Boston's luxurious Ritz-Carlton Hotel. Because the hotel was for whites only, the band members were asked to enter and exit the building through the kitchen door so as not to offend the hotel's white customers. This request greatly upset Lena's stepfather. But instead of confronting the hotel manager, he loudly blamed Sissle for accepting such a humiliating arrangement.

There may have been some merit to Mike Rodriguez's charge. But the band members did not fault Sissle, who understood the need for compromise. Instead, the band got annoyed with Mike. They felt it was easy for him to complain and then walk away from the problem because he was not black. What did he know about the concessions black Americans had to make if they wanted to get by, let alone get ahead, in society?

"With my stepfather on that bus," Lena said, "I always felt as if I was sitting with a gun that was loaded and cocked and ready to go off." Eventually, Sissle asked Mike to leave the tour, which he did. Edna, though reluctant to live apart from her husband, chose to remain with the tour and watch over Lena, who soon assumed a more prominent position in the band.

The orchestra was on its way to a gig at Moonlight Gardens in Cincinnati, Ohio, when the group found

Originally a singer and lyricist, Noble Sissle became a bandleader just as the hot sounds of jazz came into vogue in the mid-1920s. His orchestra was playing a relatively tame version of the music, however, when Horne joined his group in 1935.

out that Sissle, who was traveling separately from the band, had been injured in a car accident and would be hospitalized for a while. The engagement would make Sissle's orchestra the first black band to play in the dance hall (blacks, though, were not allowed to attend the racially segregated concert). Rather than cancel their appearance, Sissle decided to let Lena conduct the orchestra. The teenager protested, suggesting that Billy Banks would be a better choice. But Sissle was adamant. "No, Lena," he told her, "you're cuter."

The next night, the band—billed as the Noble Sissle Orchestra, directed by Helena Horne—played before an enthusiastic audience. "They had never seen anything like it before," Lena said. "I announced

Horne not only sang with Noble Sissle's Society Orchestra but also performed a tap-dance routine while dressed in a sequined outfit.

the numbers and did my songs and waved that big stick." The reviews in the local papers were excellent, and the house was filled every night.

At the age of 19, Lena was successfully supporting her family and beginning to make headway in the entertainment world. But there were some drawbacks. The demands of a life on the road allowed her little time to meet people her own age and to make friends. Her mother's vigilance only made matters worse. Edna would not let anything, including boyfriends, stand in the way of her daughter's success. As a result, Lena felt as much like a prisoner as a performer.

Lena finally escaped from her domineering mother's clutches during the Christmas season of 1936, when she went to Cleveland, Ohio, with the Sissle Orchestra. Her father came to the city to attend a boxing match between the celebrated black heavyweight champion Joe Louis and a white challenger, Johnny Risko, as well as to catch Lena's performance. When Teddy went to see his daughter backstage, he brought along his handsome traveling companion: 28-year-old Louis Jones.

A minister's son, Jones was active in Democratic party politics and was on the lookout for a proper wife. When he saw Lena, he felt his search had come to an end. She, in turn, was smitten at once by this college-educated man who was unlike anyone she knew in the entertainment world.

At Christmastime, Sissle gave his band a few weeks off, and Lena received permission from her mother to spend her holiday with her father in Pittsburgh. It was just the break Lena needed. She got to know her father's second wife, Irene, a charming and shrewd businesswoman. And she made up for lost time with Teddy. They attended parties and after-hours clubs where she saw many of his friends and acquaintances, including Louis Jones. By the end of her stay in Pittsburgh, Lena and Louis had decided to marry.

Edna strongly opposed the marriage. "It's the end of your life," she told her daughter. Sissle agreed, warning Lena that by leaving the Society Orchestra she was destroying her fledgling career. Even her father believed Louis was not the man for her. But Lena's mind was made up.

In early 1937, Lena married Louis Jones in Pittsburgh, at a small ceremony in the home of one of his brothers. The teenager defied convention by wearing a black dress. She also decided to retain her maiden name, calling herself Lena Horne-Jones. If her husband was looking for a proper and conventional wife, these two decisions should have given him pause—and they did. It quickly became apparent to the couple that they were mismatched.

Louis had old-fashioned notions regarding the role of a wife. He expected Lena to be a homemaker. She should iron shirts, cook meals, and leave the family's financial affairs to her husband. Nor should she be included when he discussed politics and social issues with his friends.

These demands were a prescription for trouble. Housework bored Lena. She preferred intelligent conversation. She had been her family's breadwinner for several years and was used to balancing checkbooks that held more money than her husband had ever seen.

The newlyweds tried to hide their mounting problems by leading a very active social life in Pittsburgh, filled with weekend parties and other events. But their high living stretched the couple's slim budget. They appealed for help to Teddy, who—as always—came through. When Lena became pregnant a few months into their marriage, the couple decided to resolve their differences for the child's sake. The baby was due in December 1937.

The months passed, and when the time came for Lena to go to the hospital, she was met in front of the building by her physician, Dr. Buster Cornelius.

He greeted her warmly and promised to see her on the following day. Then, instead of escorting the 20-year-old mother-to-be to the maternity ward, he turned around and left, knowing that black doctors were not allowed to practice in the hospital.

Lena, who was unaware of this restriction, became hysterical with fear. "I think this is perhaps the cruelest act of prejudice that was ever visited upon me personally," she later said. She was so frightened that "for two days I would not let that baby come down," she recalled. After hours of agonizing labor, a daughter, Gail, was born on December 21.

Four months later, Lena received a call from New York agent Harold Gumm, who was casting an all-black Hollywood musical film, *The Duke Is Tops*, featuring Duke Ellington and His Orchestra. Gumm told her that a costarring role in the film, opposite actor Ralph Cooper (who was known as the black Humphrey Bogart), was hers for the asking—she need not audition. The shooting schedule for the movie was only 10 days long. Lena agreed to take the job. Her family desperately needed the money.

Lena arrived in Hollywood only to learn that the producers of the movie, the Popkin brothers, had been unable to raise all of the financing for the project. This placed her salary for the film in jeopardy. When told about these developments, her husband demanded that she quit the movie and return home immediately. But she felt an obligation to the cast and crew and stayed with the project until it was completed. When the movie was released, only one number was singled out by the critics for praise: Lena's solo of "I Know You Remember."

The Duke Is Tops opened in Pittsburgh with a benefit showing for the NAACP. Lena was invited to the premiere as a guest of honor. But her husband, who still opposed Lena's show business career, would not allow her to attend the benefit.

Horne is accompanied by her first husband, Louis Jones, to the Pittsburgh airport in 1938 as she heads for Hollywood to film The Duke Is Tops.

The marriage became even more strained in the fall of 1938. Lena received another phone call from Harold Gumm, this time for a part in Lew Leslie's Broadway show *Blackbirds of 1939*. Leslie, whose *Blackbirds* revues were among New York City's most popular all-black musicals, was noted not only for discovering great black performers, including Florence Mills, but for developing their talent as well. The chance to work with Leslie was too tempting for Lena to resist.

Singer, dancer, and comedienne Florence Mills was one of the most popular black entertainers during the 1920s. A decade later, the multitalented Horne was compared to Mills by noted theater producer Lew Leslie.

Horne's many appearances on nationally broadcast radio shows—including Sunday evening performances on the "Cats 'n' Jammers" program—greatly enhanced her reputation as a singer. Ever since its early days in the 1920s, jazz has been presented to the public through remote broadcasts from nightclubs and ballrooms.

At rehearsals, Leslie brought out the best in Lena. She later said of the demanding producer that he "helped me to develop a new kind of strength. He made me feel that if I failed I would only be failing myself—not him or my mother or my husband or any of the other people I had been trying so hard to please all my life." Feeling more confident than ever before, Lena was soon swept up in the excitement that comes with creating a Broadway show.

The musical opened in New York on February 13, 1939. The reviewers, who generally have the power to make or break a show, found little to commend in *Blackbirds of 1939*. They saw only one bright spot in the entire production: Lena Horne, who was described by one observer as "a radiant songstress."

Again, Lena's husband voiced his opposition to her career. He came to New York to attend the premiere performance and then refused to let Lena go to the cast party afterward. When the show closed nine days later, she returned to Pittsburgh intent on one thing: ending her marriage.

But there was no one Lena could turn to for support. Her father did not want to see her marriage break up, and Edna and Mike had returned to Cuba. She allowed her relatives to persuade her to give the marriage one more chance. The pair reconciled, and soon Lena was pregnant with a second child, named Edwin Fletcher but called Teddy, after his grandfather. He was born in early 1940.

Sadly, Teddy's arrival did not bring his parents closer together. "I was simply using marriage—and I'm afraid Louis—to run away from a life I did not like," Lena later admitted. Her husband's attempts to control her comings and goings resembled those of her mother, but this time Lena had the confidence and the maturity to strike out on her own. She went directly to her stepmother, Irene, and borrowed some money so she could start her new life and pay someone to look after Gail and Teddy until she could send for them. Her intention was to resettle in New York, where she would look for a job.

When Lena left Pittsburgh for an unknown future, she was 23 years old and on her own for the first time in her life. But her independence did not come cheaply. Her husband, embittered by their separation, was determined to make her pay a high price for leaving. "You'll never get Teddy," he promised her. ❧

4
THE TOAST
OF THE TOWN

WHEN LENA HORNE arrived in New York City in the fall of 1940, she checked into the Theresa Hotel at 125th Street and Lenox Avenue in Harlem. The hotel, a well-known lodging place for visiting celebrities and politicians, became her home base while she looked for a singing job—any singing job— to reestablish herself in New York and put her career on the right track. Lena had already worked at the prestigious Cotton Club, acted in a Hollywood movie, appeared in two Broadway shows (to warm critical notices), and toured with a major orchestra. She had also married, given birth to two children, and separated from her husband. And she was still only 23 years old.

After taking up residence in the Theresa, Lena walked around the corner to the Apollo Theater, one of Harlem's most popular showplaces, to ask if anyone knew the whereabouts of Noble Sissle. Her problems would be solved, she thought, if she could reclaim her old job with the Society Orchestra. At the theater, Lena ran into Clarence Robinson, a former Cotton Club choreographer who was working at the Apollo. He informed her that Sissle was on the road.

Refusing to feel defeated by this information, Lena inquired about a job on the chorus line at the Apollo. Robinson told her there were no openings. Even though this ultimately turned out to be a lucky break for Horne, whose star was destined to rise much higher than that of any chorus-line hoofer, she no longer

Horne backstage during her tenure with Charlie Barnet's band, which she joined in 1940. For the first time in her career, she was allowed to perform arrangements that were specially suited to her talent.

felt very hopeful that a worthwhile opportunity would come her way. Robinson nevertheless promised to keep her in mind if he heard of any available jobs.

Lena's next step was to telephone Harold Gumm, the agent who had landed her several assignments in the past. Delighted to hear from the young singer, he helped her hunt for a spot with an orchestra. However, he could not find any gigs for her, either. Good jobs were scarce in the entertainment world, and the fact that Horne was black meant she had a slim chance at capturing a position as a singer with a well-regarded band.

Horne managed to charm the audience at Harlem's Apollo Theater during a benefit performance in 1940. Unlike the Cotton Club, the Apollo was immensely popular with the masses. Most of the acts did not meet with the audience's approval, however; the Apollo's patrons were widely known as the most demanding in New York.

Ironically, a few potential employers who *were* looking for a black singer refused to hire Horne because her facial features and light skin color made her look as though she were white. Others said she simply did not fit into the current stereotype of a black chanteuse: She did not sing the blues. One club manager even went so far as to tell Gumm that Horne should not try to make it as a black singer at all. "Let her learn a few Spanish songs, give her a Spanish name and I'll put her in," the man said.

Greatly discouraged about her job prospects, Horne soon learned that a benefit was to be presented at the Apollo Theater. She agreed to perform there even though she would not receive any money for her appearance. Perhaps, she thought, the exposure from the show would fuel her stalled career.

At the rehearsals for the Apollo benefit, Horne ran into Noble Sissle, whose band was one of several playing in the show. She asked him if he needed a singer, and when he reluctantly told her no, she felt a sharp stab of disappointment. It seemed to her as though one of her last remaining hopes for a job had just slipped away.

Yet the benefit was still to come, and there was still a chance that someone in need of a singer might spot her onstage, so Horne concentrated her energies on preparing "Yes, My Darling Daughter," "Good for Nothing Joe," and another number she had been asked to perform. Her hard work at rehearsing for the show paid off somewhat. Lena was one of the hits of the show. Much of the audience, it seemed, either remembered her from her Cotton Club days or from her stint with Sissle's orchestra. But she did not receive any job offers after the show, nor by the following afternoon.

Horne sought to forget her troubles for a while by taking in a movie at the Victoria Theater on 116th Street. Seated in the darkened theater, she was distracted by a flurry of activity at the back of the movie house. A man holding a flashlight was walking along the aisles in search of someone. It took her a moment to realize that it was Clarence Robinson from the Apollo Theater and that he was calling out her name.

Robinson had good news for Lena. Charlie Barnet was playing that night at the Windsor Theater in the Bronx, he said excitedly as he guided her out of the movie house, and one of the performers on the bill was too ill to perform. Robinson told Lena to go to the theater and try out for the job.

Lena was skeptical about her chances of hooking up with Charlie Barnet. He was widely recognized as a fine jazz musician—indeed, his recording of "Cherokee" had become a favorite in Harlem. But he was white, and Horne knew of only one other white bandleader who was willing to defy convention by hiring a black singer: clarinetist Artie Shaw, who had hired blues singer Billie Holiday for his orchestra in the spring of 1938.

Anxious to get back to work, Horne decided to follow up Robinson's suggestion immediately and meet with Barnet. She arrived at the Windsor Theater in the early evening, just as he was about to go onstage for the first show. She quickly told him why she was there, and Barnet, struck by her beauty and poise, asked her to hang around until after the band finished its first performance.

Between sets, Horne, accompanied by a pianist, sang a few songs for Barnet in a rehearsal room. His response to her was immediate. "Do you want to work in the next show?" he asked her. A few hours later, she was onstage with the Charlie Barnet Orchestra, listening to the audience applaud wildly as she finished her first song with her new band.

On the following morning, Horne moved into the Harlem YWCA at 135th Street and Seventh Avenue. Her next act was to repay her stepmother

Just like Horne, blues singer Billie Holiday rose to prominence during the 1930s as a teenager performing in Harlem night spots. They befriended one another several years later, when they were both featured at cabarets in downtown New York and attended each other's shows.

for the loan that had enabled her to move out of Pittsburgh. Then she began to save for the day when she could retrieve her children from their father and make a home for them in New York.

Horne spent most of her time with the Barnet band on the road, but the problems she encountered while touring with an all-white orchestra were quite different from those she met up with during her days with Sissle. "With Charlie," she said, "the problem was the surprise I caused." Hotels that had booked rooms in advance for Barnet and his band would claim to have no record of the reservations once the group showed up with Horne. Some hotels would grudgingly forgo their policy of racial segregation when threatened with losing the income from all of the rooms that the band had reserved. At other times, Barnet and some of the band members would leave with her and look for another hotel.

Lena with her daughter, Gail, outside their Chauncey Street home in 1941.

Finding suitable lodgings was not the only problem. At several college dances, the band was informed that the school did not want a black singer on the premises; in those cases, Lena was given a paid night off. On other occasions, she was allowed to sing with the band but had to wait somewhere else, usually in the ladies' room or on the bus, when she was not performing. Sitting with the band onstage was deemed unacceptable racial mixing.

Despite such treatment, Horne's tenure with the Charlie Barnet Orchestra resulted in a great leap forward in her artistic development. Barnet was a musician's musician: He had a great deal of respect for the natural talents of his band members. Instead of asking Horne to sound like other popular performers, he worked out arrangements specially tailored to her strengths as a vocalist. More than ever before, she was able to forge a unique personality as a singer.

After six months of performing with Barnet's orchestra, Horne was given an extended paid vacation while the rest of the band embarked on a tour of the South. Barnet, although somewhat successful in challenging the discriminatory policies of certain institutions in the northern states, did not think it was wise to travel south with his lead singer. In 1940, the South was as much a bastion of racial segregation as it had ever been.

Tired from all of the touring, Horne decided it was the perfect time to leave Barnet's band and look for a job that would allow her to bring her son and daughter to New York. She rented her grandparents' brownstone on Chauncey Street from her father, who had inherited it, and arranged for her cousin Edwina to move from Chicago to New York to help take care of the children. She then left for Pittsburgh, anxious to collect their belongings and return to Brooklyn, where they would start a new life together.

But it was not to be. Louis Jones agreed to give up custody of his daughter. "Maybe he thought it was

simply fair that the female should belong to me,"
Lena said. However, her estranged husband remained
adamant about his decision to keep Teddy. As much
as the boy's mother begged and pleaded, she could
not persuade Louis to part with his son. Finally, she
left with Gail, fully intending to return for her son
at a later date, when she was earning more money
and her negotiating position was more stable.

Although Horne was once again in search of steady
work, she had never been in a better position to look
for a job. She had already made one record that had
just become a hit—Barnet's special arrangement for
her of "Good for Nothing Joe"—and another record
that she had recently cut with Artie Shaw was about
to be released. She would soon be getting even more
exposure because Barnet had generously invited her
to sing with his orchestra at an important date at the
Paramount Theater in New York.

Noted record producer John Hammond, who had
taken part in the making of Horne's "Good for Nothing Joe," learned that she would be singing at the
Paramount. He suggested to Barney Josephson, owner
of both the Café Society Uptown and the Café Society Downtown, that he attend a matinee performance and listen to Lena. After the show concluded,
Josephson walked backstage and introduced himself
to the singer. He then asked her if she would like to
audition for a solo act at the Café Society Downtown.

The nightclub had opened on New Year's Eve in
1939 with a show featuring some of the most dynamic
talent around: Among the performers were Billie Holiday, comedian Jack Gilford, and pianist Teddy Wilson. It quickly became one of New York's most popular
and successful cabarets as well as the only totally
unsegregated night spot outside Harlem, earning it
the title of America's first political cabaret. At the
club, where the matchbook covers featured the ir-
reverent slogan *The wrong place for the Right people*,
black patrons mixed freely with whites, entertained

Blues Singer Brings Uplift
To Village's Cafe Society

Helena Horne, who is giving the Village a new thrill.

The heart of what had made Cafe Society a mecca for hep-cats and Villagers was cut out and shipped uptown last year, when the owner of the Sheridan Square bistro decided to open a second and more expensive place on 58th Street for the monied folk. The Boogie-Woogie boys, Hazel Scott and all the rest made a big financial success out of Cafe Society Uptown. But Cafe Society Downtown began to hit the skids.

Late this spring, things took a turn for the better at Cafe Society Downtown. Word had spread that Barney Josephson, presiding genius of both Cafes Society, had uncovered an exciting talent, a singer who came in as Lena Horne and stayed on as Helena Horne.

The old guard drifted back to hear Helena Horne and having heard her—and seen her—stayed. Business is better now at Cafe Society Downtown than it has been in a long time, and it's getting better. The management makes no secret of the fact that Helena is responsible for the change.

At 23, Helena Horne is snowballing to fame, as a beautiful blues singer and a singer with a beautiful blues style. She now is featured on the "Cats 'n' Jammers" program over WOR (Sunday, 6-6:30 p.m.) and bands from Duke Ellington down are dickering for her services. Her *Summertime* is becoming a Cafe Society *specialité de la maison*.

New York's Café Society Downtown started to lose customers to its sister club shortly after owner Barney Josephson opened an uptown cabaret in 1940. The situation changed, however, once the 23-year-old Horne began performing at the Greenwich Village night spot. According to this article in PM, a New York newspaper, "She is snowballing to fame . . . and bands from Duke Ellington down are dickering for her services."

by a galaxy of newly discovered talents, including actor Zero Mostel and pianist Hazel Scott.

Horne began her audition with Josephson by asking Teddy Wilson to accompany her on "Sleepy Time

Down South." Her choice of songs shocked Josephson. To Lena, "Sleepy Time Down South" was simply a pleasant tune about the good life in the South. But not to Josephson. "Do you know what you're singing?" he asked her. Did she really believe that life in the South was as idyllic as the song made it out to be?

Admittedly, Horne had never thought of songs in such a context. "During my middle-class interludes in Brooklyn, and in Harlem," she said in her autobiography, "we had been so preoccupied by our particular brand of Northern-style misery that we thought little of the lot of the Southern Negro." Her musical education under the tutelage of Barney Josephson had just begun.

With the club owner as her guide, Lena—once again billed as Helena Horne—opened to rave reviews early in the spring of 1941. Josephson selected all of her songs, which included "The Man I Love," "Summertime," and Billie Holiday's blues song "Fine and Mellow." Earlier in her career, Horne had never sung the blues. But now, with Josephson as her mentor, she learned how to project into her songs the deep feelings that lie at the heart of such music.

Never settling for less than the best, Josephson continued to work with Horne after her engagement began. He stressed the importance of listening to and feeling every word of a song, at one point advising her to think of her children when performing the sentimental tune "Summertime." The first time Lena did this during a show, she got so caught up in her emotions that she unwittingly heaved a deep sigh in the middle of the tune. The enraptured audience responded instantly, bursting into a round of applause.

Horne's solo act quickly became an unqualified hit, breaking all attendance records at Café Society Downtown and bringing in a constant stream of repeat business. It was not unusual for fans to see the show four or five times. Unable to land a singing job only a short time before, Lena was fast becoming the toast of the town, earning a hefty $75 a week.

Horne cashed in on her sudden success. She began to perform regularly on radio broadcasts, and she signed a solo recording contract with RCA Victor. Her first album, released in 1941, included "I Gotta Right to Sing the Blues" and "Moanin' Low."

For Horne, the seven-month stint at the cabaret had much more to offer her than the usual benefits of a well-received singing engagement. The club proved to be a meeting ground for black artists and intellectuals—including bandleader Duke Ellington; singer-

Horne and jazz pianist Hazel Scott (left) were two of the top attractions at Barney Josephson's Café Society. Lena generally starred at the downtown bistro, on Sheridan Square, although she sometimes substituted for Scott at the club on 58th Street.

Duke Ellington, playing here for a group of servicemen, was one of many celebrated black artists who frequented the Café Society Downtown while Horne was headlining there. "I could see him being paid homage by the white people in the audience at the Café," Horne said of the noted bandleader and composer, "and his greatness enveloped the performers—we were all in his orbit."

actor Paul Robeson; Walter White, the executive secretary of the NAACP; and educator and politician Ralph Bunche—and while performing there she met these and other luminaries. Many of them were friends of her uncle Frank's, who was often in New York on goverment business. He worked in Washington, D.C., as an official on federal housing programs and served on President Franklin D. Roosevelt's black cabinet, an informal presidential advisory board that focused on the special needs of black citizens.

Lena's engagement at Café Society Downtown ultimately led her into a period of tremendous social awakening. Her new friends and acquaintances (especially Paul Robeson, who told her, "You are a

Horne first met singer-actor Paul Robeson in 1940, at the Café Society Downtown. He was deeply involved in racial issues and helped spur Lena's interest in civil rights matters.

Negro—and that is the whole basis of what you are and what you will become") saw to it that she received a wide-ranging political and cultural education. She consequently developed a deep interest in agitating for black civil rights.

With her solo act a huge success and her social conscience raised to new heights, the 24-year-old entertainer could also claim she was happier in her personal life than ever before. She had both of her children with her because her former husband had allowed Teddy to come to Brooklyn for an extended stay. Her uncle Frank visited her regularly, as did her uncle Burke, who had become manager of the Apollo Theater. In addition, she was involved in a secret love affair, brief but exciting, with a man whom she once described as the "one invincible Negro . . . who carried so many of our hopes, maybe even dreams of vengeance": the celebrated boxer Joe Louis.

Late in the summer of 1941, Harold Gumm contacted Horne after receiving a call from Felix Young, a well-known composer who was planning to open a new nightclub in Los Angeles called the Trocadero. Young had already signed up some of the biggest stars in the black entertainment world for the club's first show: Ethel Waters, Duke Ellington and His Orchestra, and the Katherine Dunham Dance Company. He also wanted to sign up Horne.

Young's offer left Horne confused. If she accepted it, she would have to leave the old brownstone in Brooklyn, uproot her newly settled family, and give up a secure job for a prestigious but nevertheless fledgling enterprise. On the other hand, performing at the Trocadero would give her a chance to work with some of the best black artists in the country.

Frank Horne renewed his relationship with Lena shortly after he became director of the Office of Race Relations for the U.S. Housing Authority, a position that frequently brought him to New York on government business. He is shown here standing to the right of Mary McLeod Bethune, the first black woman to be placed in charge of a federal agency. They are flanked by other members of President Franklin Roosevelt's administration.

Horne plays a duet with heavyweight champion Joe Louis. They became reacquainted in the spring of 1941, during a visit arranged by Lena's father.

Walter White, head of the nation's most influential civil rights organization, urged her to go. He stressed that a performer as sophisticated as she was could be a pioneer in Hollywood. By working in the heart of America's entertainment industry, which was controlled entirely by whites, she could become an inspiration to other black performers and show that blacks were more than base comedians and shuffling servants. She ultimately decided—over Barney Josephson's staunch objections—to leave her engagement at Café Society Downtown and head for the West Coast.

In the fall of 1941, Horne boarded a transcontinental train—the shiny, silver Twentieth Century Limited—with her cousin Edwina and her three-and-a-half-year-old daughter, Gail. The journey westward was to be quite unlike the train trips of Lena's childhood, when she and her mother were forced to ride in crowded, uncomfortable Jim Crow cars. The landmark Supreme Court ruling in *Mitchell* v. *U.S. Interstate Commerce Act*, which had been handed down earlier in the year, required all railroad companies to provide equal accommodations for blacks. As a result, the three travelers shared a well-appointed compartment on the train.

The Twentieth Century Limited departed from New York City's Grand Central Station at dinnertime and pulled into Chicago just as its passengers were waking in the early morning hours. There the threesome changed trains. They boarded the celebrated Super Chief, which raced along the plains of the Midwest, then crossed the long stretches of western desert, and finally arrived at the lush orange groves of southern California, where Lena hoped to break new ground. **◆**

Walter White, the executive secretary of the National Association for the Advancement of Colored People, encouraged Horne to use her growing fame to set an inspiring example of achievement for other black performers. Like many of the nation's most prominent civil rights activists, he had been a friend of Lena's grandmother's.

5
WOMAN OF THE YEAR

❧

A FEW DAYS after Lena Horne arrived on the West Coast, she received word that the opening of the Trocadero was going to be delayed indefinitely because of financing problems. To make matters worse, Duke Ellington and Ethel Waters pulled out of the all-star lineup. The very reasons that had compelled her to uproot her family and test the waters in California were beginning to disappear.

Horne awaited the highly touted opening of the Trocadero mostly by remaining in her Los Angeles apartment (located on the appropriately named Horn Avenue). Occasionally, she kept company with Katherine Dunham and her dancers, who were also biding their time. But for the most part she felt alone and missed her friends in New York.

One day, Horne discovered that Duke Ellington was also in Los Angeles, appearing in the revue *Jump for Joy*, a celebration of black life in America. In devising the musical arrangements for this show, he had collaborated, as he did for most of his career, with composer and pianist Billy Strayhorn, whose many compositions included the jazz classics "Take

Several factors helped Horne become America's first black sex symbol. Among them were her natural beauty, the exquisite gowns she wore, and the intimate setting of the cabarets where she performed romantic songs.

the A Train" and "Lush Life." Back at the Café Society Downtown, Ellington had constantly urged Lena to get to know his right-hand man. "You and he need to know each other," she was told. But the two had never found the time to meet.

In Los Angeles, Ellington finally engineered the meeting. He invited Horne to attend *Jump for Joy*, offering her a front-row seat at the sold-out, standing-room-only performance. When she arrived at the theater and settled into her spot, she noticed that a seat next to hers was empty. It remained unoccupied even after the lights dimmed and the show began.

At the intermission, a small, beautifully dressed man sat down next to Lena and introduced himself as Billy Strayhorn. True to Ellington's prediction, she and Strayhorn became fast friends. "When we were together," she said later, ". . . we seemed sometimes almost siblings."

On a bright Sunday afternoon in late 1941, Horne was rehearsing some new song arrangements with

Arranger Billy Strayhorn (left), Duke Ellington's right-hand man, collaborated with the bandleader and composer for 28 years. Strayhorn also became an indispensable companion to Horne, as Ellington had once predicted he would.

Strayhorn when they heard the news that shocked the entire nation: The Japanese had attacked the U.S. naval base at Pearl Harbor, Hawaii. Five days later, on December 12, the United States formally entered World War II, and the country geared up for the war effort.

Felix Young had come close to completing the financing of the Trocadero, but the wartime restrictions that were subsequently introduced prevented him from obtaining the materials he needed to build his new club. His dream of establishing a premier nightclub in Los Angeles collapsed. Yet he refused to give up. With the limited funds he had left, he opened a small night spot on the Sunset Strip that he called the Little Troc. Lena Horne and the Katherine Dunham Dance Company, holdovers from Young's all-star lineup at the Trocadero, headlined the opening bill.

The small stage proved to be a nightmare for the Dunham dancers. Although their routines were beautifully choreographed, the dances looked like traffic jams at rush hour because the performance area was so cramped. Front-row patrons had their drinks swept off the tables by the dancers' flowing costumes. Within three days, the dance troupe quit.

But the intimate room was perfect for Horne. Her act, which was fairly similar to her successful Café Society show, featured several arrangements by Billy Strayhorn, including "Blues in the Night" and "Honeysuckle Rose." And like her New York stage presentation, it was an overnight sensation. "People who never went to night clubs pushed their way into the place four or five nights a week," reported a *New York Times* correspondent.

In fact, the Little Troc quickly became the in place for Hollywood's top movie stars; Lana Turner, Marlene Dietrich, and Greta Garbo were among the most renowned visitors to the nightclub. Horne, a

Dancer and choreographer Katherine Dunham specialized in African and Caribbean rhythms and movements while sharing the bill with Horne at the Little Troc in Los Angeles. She later became the first black choreographer to work at the Metropolitan Opera in New York City.

local newspaper duly noted, "has knocked the movie population bowlegged and is up to her ears in offers." Just as NAACP leader Walter White had predicted, she was well on her way to becoming a pioneer in the entertainment world.

The first film studio to court Horne was one of Hollywood's biggest: Metro-Goldwyn-Mayer (MGM). One of the studio's executives, producer Arthur Freed, was so impressed with Lena's rendition of "More Than You Know" during her audition at the studio that he immediately phoned Louis B. Mayer, the head of MGM, and asked if he had time to listen to a new star. Within minutes, Horne was whisked across the movie lot and escorted into the spacious office of one of the most powerful men in town.

A rather stubby man whose explosive moods were legendary throughout the industry, Mayer assumed a paternal attitude toward Horne. He sat at his desk, with his hands clasped in front of him, listening to her sing. By the end of her performance, the movie mogul was absolutely enthralled. He talked excitedly about *Cabin in the Sky*, an all-black Broadway musical whose movie rights MGM had recently bought. Although filming of the hit show was not slated to begin for some time, casting for the production had already begun. One of the leading roles, he told Lena, had yet to be filled.

A few days later, MGM offered Horne a seven-year contract that would guarantee her a starring role in *Cabin in the Sky*. Faced with the prospect of signing a multiyear contract at a time when there were no blacks under long-term contracts at any of the major Hollywood studios, she consulted the people she trusted most: her family and friends. Her father traveled to Los Angeles to attend Lena's next meeting at the studio. Nattily dressed as always, he took command of the conference room. "I have very few illusions about the movie business," he told the studio executives. "The only Negroes I ever see are menials or Tarzan extras. I don't see what the movies have to offer my daughter. I can hire a maid for her; why should she act one?"

Walter White also happened to be in town while Horne's contract with MGM was being negotiated. He was similarly concerned that she would be forced to play demeaning roles while waiting for production to begin on *Cabin in the Sky*. He told her, "It is essential that you establish a new kind of image for black women," and she heeded his advice during her contract talks.

The studio executives listened intently to Lena and her father express their views on how she should be handled. Finally, Mayer gave them his personal assurance that absolutely nothing would be done to embarrass the new starlet, and the breakthrough contract was signed. The agreement included provisions designed to shield Lena from racial segregation. Among them was a clause that called for her, whenever on studio business, to stay only in hotels that would allow her to use the front door.

Next came Horne's first screen test: a comic love scene taken from the script of a film in which she was tabbed to appear with radio star Eddie ("Rochester") Anderson. The makeup department, in an attempt to match her skin color to that of the darker-skinned Anderson, smeared so much dark foundation on her that she looked as if she were a white person trying to play the part in blackface—a reminder of Hollywood's inglorious past, when so many of the roles calling for black characters were played by made-up whites. Cosmetics expert Max Factor was called in to rescue the situation but could offer little help. The screen test was a total disaster, and Horne lost the part to Ethel Waters.

One other consequence of the ill-fated screen test proved to be even more disturbing. Max Factor worked with his chemists to create for Horne a caramel-colored pancake makeup base that was applied with a wet sponge; the color, which was supposed to make Lena's skin look darker, was dubbed Light Egyptian. But the special makeup was not reserved only for Horne. The studio bosses also used it on leading white actresses so they could star in roles that called for black women. Because of this makeup, black actresses—including Horne, who lost the lead part in *Showboat* to Ava Gardner—continued to be bypassed for major roles. White actresses were cast instead.

One reason blacks such as Horne were not given starring roles was that the film industry feared that as soon as a few blacks gained some status, many more would begin to agitate for better acting assignments. This line of reasoning certainly haunted Horne. Her outspoken views and insistent contract demands threatened the firmly entrenched casting system that

hired black extras—actors who populate the screen in crowd scenes but do not have any scripted dialogue—and ultimately involved her in a great deal of conflict.

The controversy was orchestrated, oddly enough, by a small but elite group of black Hollywood actors. When a studio needed black extras, it contacted one of the members of this unofficial group, who in turn told other blacks about the job openings. Accordingly, an extra's chances at employment depended upon the goodwill of these work leaders, who were rewarded by the studios for their casting efforts by being offered the best acting roles of all.

Fearful of Horne's motives, the members of this casting community called a protest meeting that she attended. There she was accused of attempting to put

While becoming a part of Hollywood's film industry, Horne took an active role in campaigning for black rights. "I was in a rare position for a Negro," she said. "I could do something—even if it was only a little bit—about discrimination."

them all out of work by refusing to appear in the kinds of films—"jungle" and "plantation" movies—that provided Hollywood's blacks with the bulk of their roles. They called her "a tool of the NAACP" and left her very much confused by their assaults. "The one thing I had not expected," she said of her entrance into Hollywood, "was to get into trouble with my own race."

Paul Robeson instructed her not to pay any attention to these protests. "It's . . . the people farther down the line—whose opinion of you really matters," he said. Another of her supporters was Hattie McDaniel, the first black to win an Academy Award for acting (for her portrayal of Scarlett O'Hara's slave in *Gone with the Wind*). She said to Lena, "You have to do what's right for you."

In the meantime, the studio heads at MGM could not decide on a role for Horne to play. Finally, they

Horne and pianist Hazel Scott were accompanied by a choral group and a full orchestra for their grand musical number in I Dood It! *During the making of this film, Horne, as MGM's leading black actress, saw the studio raise her salary to $900 per week.*

bowed to pressure from Paul Robeson and Walter White, who were repeatedly asking them when they were going to put Lena in a film, and added an extra musical number to the film version of Cole Porter's hit Broadway musical *Panama Hattie*. Lena, singing "Just One of Those Things," was featured in the new number, dressed in an attractive gown and wearing a white gardenia in her hair.

The movie, starring Red Skelton and Ann Sothern, was released in 1942 and seemed to be a triumph for the MGM executives. By featuring Horne in an extra scene in *Panama Hattie*, the studio heads not only silenced some of their critics but also managed to keep all of their distributors satisfied. They had arranged Lena's scene so that her appearance had nothing to do with the story line of the movie. Thus, the studio was able to cut out the scene for any distributor—especially those in the South—who refused to handle a movie that showed blacks in other than subservient roles. In spite of this strategy, Lena's appearance in *Panama Hattie* was the only well-received part of the movie, and fan mail started to pour into the studio's offices.

Horne's next movie, *Thousands Cheer*, was an all-star musical whose cast included entertainers Gene Kelly and Judy Garland. This time, Lena was given two big production numbers: "Honeysuckle Rose" and "Brazilian Boogie." Asked to do little else, she began to tire of her entire Hollywood experience, despite the growing public acclaim that came her way. She had always had reservations about pursuing a film career, and now she was more skeptical than ever. When she heard that a big benefit was scheduled at Café Society Downtown, she decided to fly east and attend.

The moment Horne's plane touched down in New York, she realized how much she had missed being there. She made the rounds of all her familiar haunts and visited with her friends Billy Strayhorn, Charlie Barnet, and Barney Josephson. But instead of making her feel better, the trip only underscored how miserable and out of place she felt in Los Angeles.

On the final night of her New York visit, Horne tearfully told bandleader Count Basie, another friend from her Café Society days, that she did not want to go back to Hollywood. She did not want to become a film star.

Basie's response was immediate and electric. "They," he said, meaning whites, "never choose us, but they've chosen you. You have to go back so that other people can have your opportunities. Nobody's ever had this chance before."

Others had said similar things to her in the past, but Basie's words struck a different chord. "What I took away from my encounter with him," she said later, "was the knowledge that this was the kind of a favor you prove yourself worthy of only after it is given . . . the way you use it is the important thing, not the question of whether you really deserved it in the first place." The next day, she flew back to California.

Cabin in the Sky, Horne's next movie assignment, was still not ready to go into production. Instead, she and Hazel Scott, who was usually performing at the Café Society Uptown when Lena was working at the downtown club, recorded a complicated version of "Joshua Fit the Battle of Jericho" for *I Dood It!*, another Red Skelton film. Music arranger Kay Thompson wanted to call in MGM staff composer and arranger Lennie Hayton to inject some energy into the recording, but he was tied up with another studio project, so they continued with the number as planned. The recording was matched to a film sequence several months later.

Thompson was not only an arranger but also the studio's vocal coach, and she helped the 25 year old improve her singing by teaching her the mechanics of breath control. Lena already had impeccable diction—the result of her grandmother constantly reminding her to articulate clearly whenever she spoke and of her work with Sissle, Leslie, and Josephson. But as a singer Lena did not project her voice as well as Thompson thought she should. Her singing lessons with Thompson remedied this and also had an enormous impact on Lena's vocal range, enabling her to hit notes she had never reached before.

The results of Horne's labors soon paid off. Still waiting for *Cabin in the Sky* to begin shooting, she accepted an offer to work at the Mocambo. Like the Little Troc, it was a nightclub along the Sunset Strip, and Lena's floor show there was a tremendous success. One critic reported after catching her act in the summer of 1942, "We heard a great singer who is something more than that—a great actress; and something more than that, I suspect—a great soul."

Horne with Eddie ("Rochester") Anderson (left) and Rex Ingram on the set of Cabin in the Sky. *They are rehearsing a scene in which Lena is supposed to lure Anderson from his wife.*

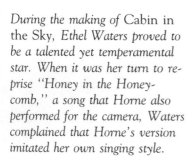

During the making of Cabin in the Sky, *Ethel Waters proved to be a talented yet temperamental star. When it was her turn to reprise "Honey in the Honeycomb," a song that Horne also performed for the camera, Waters complained that Horne's version imitated her own singing style.*

At last, shooting began on *Cabin in the Sky.* Vincente Minnelli, who had directed Horne's first two MGM films, was once again in charge; Roger Edens was the musical director; and Eddie Anderson, Katherine Dunham, and Duke Ellington and His Orchestra were in the cast. All told, the group resembled one big, happy family—except for one member: Ethel Waters, who had achieved stardom at a great personal cost. Her long and arduous rise to the top had caused her to become distrustful and a difficult person with whom to work. Many well-known black performers, including Billie Holiday and Katherine Dunham, had been the target of her wrath. So it did not surprise many people when Waters began to view Horne as a rival, a young upstart who had not yet paid her dues.

There was no way for Horne to avoid a confrontation with Waters: The film's story line called for one. *Cabin in the Sky* is about the struggle between a good wife and the devil's temptress for the soul of the woman's wayward husband. The finale, set in a nightclub, is a showdown between the sympathetic woman, the character played by Waters, and Horne's wicked temptress, Georgia Brown.

Horne chipped a bone in her ankle while practicing a dance routine just one day before the nightclub sequence was to be filmed. Waters had put a hex on Horne, Anderson joked. But for Lena it was no laughing matter. Her ankle had to be put into a plaster cast, and the camera angles for the finale had to be reworked so that the cast was hidden from view.

The next morning, Horne hobbled onto the set, ready to shoot her scene with Waters. Lena had already been advised by the director: "Be real small. You can never be stronger than Ethel." Yet she got a big laugh when she recited her very first line of the finale, upstaging Waters. Then a propman brought her a pillow to put under her injured ankle. Waters, angered by the attention being given to the young starlet, went into a tirade. She berated Horne for what she called a lack of talent and went on to blast everyone on the set. Shooting had to be suspended for the rest of the day. When it resumed, the cast and crew pretended that nothing had happened. But Waters and Horne never spoke to one another again.

Stormy Weather, the picture that Horne was supposed to make after *Cabin in the Sky*, was not scheduled to begin filming right away, so in November 1942 she returned to the East Coast for a brief run at New York's Savoy-Plaza Hotel. Shortly after the engagement began, a reporter for *Newsweek* said of her act, "Any member of her nightly SRO [standing-room only] audience at the Savoy-Plaza Café Lounge will testify . . . that she knows how to sell a song."

Horne with bandleader and composer Fats Waller (left) in a scene from Stormy Weather. She "digs deep into the depths of romantic despair to put across the classic blues number," the New York Times said of Lena's rendition of the title song, ". . . in a manner that is distinctive and refreshing."

Horne's appearance at the Savoy-Plaza was a breakthrough engagement on two counts: No solo act had ever before played the hotel's prestigious Café Lounge, nor had any black performed there before Lena. Nevertheless, the hotel's managers refused to let her break all of its racial barriers. They gave her a suite where she could change and rest between shows, but they would not allow her to stay in the hotel overnight.

One night shortly after the engagement opened to rave reviews, Horne collapsed onstage. She was carried upstairs to her suite, where a doctor pronounced her too ill to be moved. The Savoy-Plaza's management, not wanting to alienate her because she was making a lot of money for the hotel, told her she could remain in the suite overnight. But Lena refused to stay. "I don't care if I'm dying," she said. "Don't leave me where I'm not wanted." She had her accompanist drive her to the Theresa Hotel in Harlem.

The following night, a proud Horne returned to the show and its usual capacity house. She became such a sensation that during the week of January 9, 1943, three of the nation's best-known magazines— *Life, Newsweek,* and *Time*—ran feature-length articles on her. "When Lena sings at dinner and supper, forks are halted in mid-career," *Time* reported. "She seethes her songs with the air of a bashful volcano." So much attention and praise was a publicity agent's dream come true.

Horne returned to Hollywood in early 1943 and went right to work on *Stormy Weather*, which co-starred Bill ("Bojangles") Robinson, Cab Calloway, and Fats Waller. Lena had already sung the title song, a classic blues number, in her club act, and now she added the film version of the song to her growing list of credits. When the movie was released in 1943, "Stormy Weather" promptly became her trademark song.

Stormy Weather, in an unexpected run of good luck and impeccable timing, opened within months of *Thousands Cheer* and *Cabin in the Sky*. Reaching the public right on the heels of her publicity blitz in the national press, it helped her, at age 26, become one of the best-known black entertainers in America. The year was only half over, yet Lena Horne was already the hottest story of 1943. ❧

6

"VERY FIERY,
VERY STRONG"

Horne's growing fame as an actress coincided with the advent of World War II. She is shown here entertaining servicemen at a Hollywood Canteen show.

AFTER RETURNING TO New York City in 1943 for the premiere of *Cabin in the Sky*, Horne began a week-long engagement at the prestigious Howard Theater in Washington, D.C. The show did not draw well at first. A rising star, Lena commanded a hefty salary, which caused the theater's management to charge a fairly high price for her act. Thus, many of the area's blacks were unable to afford tickets to the show. Once she found out how expensive the seats were, she took a cut in salary so more people could come to the theater.

While Horne was endearing herself to wartime Washington, she was also winning the hearts of America's black GI's on two fronts: as an entertainer and as a black activist. They prized Lena for her sex appeal and good looks and decorated their barracks with MGM publicity posters of her. Screenings of *Cabin in the Sky* and *Stormy Weather* proved to be extremely popular with the black troops. She was so revered by them, in fact, that when one black soldier said, "Some people fought the war for Dwight Eisenhower, but I fought it for Lena Horne," others surely must have felt the same way.

Horne was so loved by her admirers that she was often treated like royalty when she went to entertain the troops. One of her stops was the Tuskegee Institute in Tuskegee, Alabama—the only training school in the country for black combat pilots. According to poet Sterling Brown, who happened to be at the institute when she arrived, the place immediately went wild. As she watched the school's first group of aviators graduate to the 99th Pursuit Squadron, the men eagerly proclaimed her the "Queen of the 99th."

Horne's wartime charity work included tours with two different outfits: the Hollywood Canteen and the United Service Organizations (USO). It was during these entertainment cavalcades that she began to speak out in public on topics that were very important to her, especially the issue of civil rights in the armed forces. Although black GI's in the United States were asked to give their life for their country, they were kept in segregated units, with little chance of being promoted to officer. "The basic, terrible irony was plain to see," she said in her autobiography. "Here were Negro men drafted to fight for their country—for freedom, if you will—and forced to accept the discipline and customs of a Jim Crow Army."

While working for the USO, Horne was asked to follow the organization's practice of entertaining blacks and whites separately. "I was always expected to entertain the white soldiers first," she said, "then the Negroes—and often under the most degrading conditions for both the soldiers and me." She did not

America's first group of black fighter pilots, the 99th Pursuit Squadron, dubbed Horne "Queen of the 99th" during her visit to their training school in Tuskegee, Alabama. Her professional appearances gave the black troops, she said, "a respite from the special hell to which they were assigned."

appreciate this arrangement, and the last straw for her came during a show at Camp Robertson, Arkansas, when she went to the mess hall to entertain the black troops. Instead of seeing black soldiers only, she saw a group of white men occupying the front-row seats, with the black soldiers seated behind them. Because she had entertained the white troops the night before, she asked a stagehand who these men were. She was told they were German prisoners of war.

"I don't think I have ever been more furious in my life," Horne said. She walked off the stage and demanded to be taken to the nearest NAACP office so she could lodge a formal protest about the army's treatment of black soldiers. The NAACP representative at the small local office was a young woman named Daisy Bates (who in 1957 would rise to national prominence as the courageous leader of the Arkansas NAACP during Little Rock's Central High School integration crisis). She and Lena wired a complaint to the Hollywood branch of the USO, which in turn censured Horne for her failure to perform. She was, in effect, kicked out of the organization for pointing out that the German prisoners of war were treated better than the U.S. Army's own soldiers.

For the duration of the war, Horne avoided the USO and performed for black troops at her own expense. Her political involvement extended to other civil rights activities as well. She served on the board of the Hollywood Independent Citizens' Committee of the Arts, Sciences, and Professions; actively promoted the Fair Employment Practices Commission in California; and worked for the Hollywood Victory Committee, which was spearheaded by actress Bette Davis.

Horne was clearly following in the footsteps of her socially conscious grandmother. In fact, she was very much like Cora, Paul Robeson told her: "Very fiery, very strong." It was a point with which Lena

Horne's refusal to perform in Arkansas at a USO show that encouraged racial discrimination (the black GI's in attendance were seated behind white German prisoners of war) ultimately led to a meeting with NAACP representative Daisy Bates, who emerged years later as one of the nation's foremost civil rights leaders.

Edwina, a second cousin, and Horne's daughter, Gail, outside their home in Los Angeles.

agreed, admitting that she had learned from her grandmother "not to take any nonsense from anybody." And now that she had reached a certain level of prestige, she was ready to speak out and be heard. She began, she said, "to look for . . . fights."

Horne soon found one, literally in her own backyard. She moved with Gail and Edwina (Teddy soon joined them as well) to a Mexican-style, two-family home that was just down the block on Horn Avenue. Within days of settling in her new home, she discovered that a few neighbors were circulating a petition to have her move because she was black. But before Lena could act, the matter was resolved. Thanks to the efforts of some very prominent neighbors, including actors Humphrey Bogart and Peter Lorre, the petition disappeared.

Horne's return to Hollywood allowed her to pursue a relationship with fellow MGM employee Lennie Hayton. She first heard about him while she was working on *I Dood It!*, and in the months that followed, they ran into one another several times at the studio commissary where everyone lunched and at parties. Their relationship evolved from one of polite disregard to serious involvement.

Hayton was originally trained as a classical pianist but turned his attention to the sounds of jazz while in his teens. He joined Paul Whiteman's orchestra as a pianist-arranger and played alongside the likes of cornetist Bix Beiderbecke, trombonists Jack Teagarden and Tommy Dorsey, and clarinetist and saxophonist Jimmy Dorsey. He later worked on live radio broadcasts as music director of both the "Fred Allen Show" orchestra and the "Hit Parade" orchestra, which reprised the top pop tunes of the week.

Edwina, Lena's longtime companion and helper, refused to accept the budding relationship between her cousin and Lennie Hayton because he was white. She vehemently proclaimed that Lena was going to

ruin her career if she kept carrying on with someone who was not black. Tensions came to a head when Edwina demanded that Lena choose between her and Lennie. Lena opted for the man she had come to love, and Edwina moved out of the house shortly thereafter.

Lena soon moved away as well. When Gail and Teddy became the targets of racial prejudice at their Los Angeles school, she decided to return with her family to New York. She bought a house in St. Albans, in the borough of Queens, and hired a woman named Ida Sparks to look after her children.

The family did not remain intact, however. Horne's divorce from Louis Jones was finally formalized in 1944, after years of separation, and the court man-

Composer and arranger Lennie Hayton conducts Horne during a rehearsal. "After I met Lennie," she said, "I gradually stopped being a girl who happened to sing for her living and began to be a woman who derived part of her identity from her profession."

dated that Louis retain custody of Teddy. From that time forward, she saw her son only a few months out of the year and had to rely on lawyers and accountants to follow his progress.

Horne's move to the East Coast did little damage to her career, for it had become apparent that MGM did not intend to make much use of her. Between 1942, when she finished up *I Dood It!*, and 1945, she appeared in musical sequences in only a few more films: *Swing Fever*, *Broadway Rhythm*, *Two Girls and a Sailor*, and *Ziegfeld Follies*. Filming these sequences, which were cut out of the movies when they were screened in the South, took no more than a few weeks of her time. The studio executives knew they had a popular, talented black performer under contract, but they did not know what to do with her. America, they felt, was not ready to accept an educated black film star who would not mug for the camera.

Horne's role in Ziegfeld Follies, an all-star extravaganza, was further evidence, she said, that the whites who ran Hollywood "advised me to forget the basic fact of my color." This scene was later cut from the movie.

Having virtually no other choice, Horne took to the road—a decision that pleased MGM's executives, who were happy to see her gain exposure. She performed in clubs and theaters throughout the country, including the Chez Paree in Chicago, as she refined her solo act and left new attendance records in her wake. At this point in her career, Lena later recalled, she "was beginning to be a good entertainer. I was beginning to have a sense of my own presence on stage—and I was beginning to sense that audiences could respond to that."

Evidence of her growing fame appeared in October 1944, when a stunning photograph of Lena Horne, bejeweled and as elegant as ever, graced the cover of *Motion Picture* magazine. It was the first time a black star appeared on the cover. Readers responded to the cover and its accompanying article with a deluge of congratulatory mail.

Horne was profiled in other periodicals as well, including the Los Angeles *Sentinel*, a black newspaper that reported, "Besides beauty, she has brains—and she uses them," and *Movieland*, which called her "a forthright and intelligent champion of her people." But her appearance on the cover of *Sensación*, a popular Cuban magazine, created a response in one particular reader that she had not counted on: Her mother, Edna, saw the cover and flew from her home in Havana to visit her daughter in Hollywood, eager to resurrect her acting career by using her daughter's connections.

Upon her arrival in California, Lena's mother checked into a whites-only hotel in Los Angeles. Because Lena was not allowed on the hotel grounds, Lennie picked up Edna and drove her to a meeting with Lena, who tried to explain that she wielded no real power in the industry and would not be able to help her mother land an acting job. Edna refused to believe her daughter and threatened to regale news-

The October 1944 issue of Motion Picture magazine reported that Horne was "the only colored actress who has sustained a career in Hollywood without being a comedy character or portraying servants. . . . Her great ambition is to use her talent and success to win respect for her people."

Lena with her mother in 1944, at a tea held in Los Angeles by the National Council of Negro Women.

paper columnists with tales of her ungrateful, spiteful daughter. Only after Lena agreed to increase the monthly stipends that she wired to her mother and stepfather did she persuade Edna to return to Cuba.

In 1945, Hayton and Horne worked together for the first time on a movie. The project was *Till the Clouds Roll By*, an MGM film biography of songwriter Jerome Kern. It featured yet another musical sequence during which Lena, costumed in an elegant, flowing gown, performed a song while leaning against a pillar. The film, which boasted singers Judy Garland and Frank Sinatra, was an all-star flop.

Because Horne was cast in the same role in every movie MGM asked her to make, she felt that she and the studio executives had reached an impasse in their business relationship. That same year, she had turned down the starring role in *St. Louis Woman*, a Broadway musical produced by Arthur Freed, despite extreme pressure from the studio that she accept it. Lena firmly believed that the play perpetuated negative black stereotypes, and she said so to the people at MGM. From that moment on, the studio refused to give her permission to perform in nightclubs and theaters, in effect punishing her for the strength of her convictions.

Horne, who in addition to her New York residence had just bought a small home in the Nichols Canyon section of Los Angeles, was hurt financially by this ban. But she was also deprived of something else: Working in the cabarets had stretched her as an artist. She tried to compensate for the missed club dates by working hard at improving her vocal skills, just as she had done with Kay Thompson.

Up to this point in her career, Horne had always been touted as a great performer with an uncanny ability to sell a song. The pure sound of her voice, however, had never been put in the same class as jazz singer Ella Fitzgerald's or blues singer Billie Holiday's.

So, with Hayton's help, she focused on enriching her voice and working on more interesting and challenging musical arrangements. When the time came for her to return to the stage, the audience would undoubtedly discover that she was more in command as a performer than ever before.

After months of enforced idleness, Horne made a virtually unprecedented move in Hollywood. She arranged a direct talk with studio head Louis B. Mayer in an effort to remedy her situation. The interview, held in Mayer's office, was emotionally charged, but it paid off. Horne was allowed to work again, although her relationship with the studio remained strained and was never totally mended.

Horne was more fiery than ever when she returned to the nightclub scene in 1945. Confident of her abilities, she began to make strict demands at some of her engagements. During her record-breaking, sold-out run at the Copacabana in New York, she discovered that blacks were not being allowed to see the show. Their reservations were gladly accepted by the management, but when they showed up at the club, they were told that all records of their reservations had "mysteriously" disappeared. Lena was infuriated when she learned about this, and from that time on, she would not work at a cabaret unless there was a nondiscrimination clause in her contract guaranteeing that people of every race had a right to attend the show.

When Horne returned to the Copacabana the following year, blacks watched from the audience as her backup band was led by a new conductor: Lennie Hayton. He had taken a leave of absence from MGM so he could come to the East Coast with her. Although they had not yet mentioned it to anyone, marriage loomed in their plans.

On August 21, 1947, Horne attended a celebration of a different sort: Lena Horne Day had been

Horne's two children—Gail, age nine, and Teddy, age seven—during a visit to New York.

Although Horne was featured prominently in films such as Broadway Rhythm, *she had a hard time landing challenging roles. "I was forever living up to someone else's idea of what I should be, who I should be," she said.*

formally declared in Brooklyn. The 30-year-old entertainer was escorted through the streets of her old neighborhood in a special motorcade as crowds stood along the way and applauded her return home. At the official ceremonies, she was given a citation from Girls High School, which honored her as one of its "distinguished daughters."

As Horne smiled and waved to her fans, she wondered how many of them would approve of the decision she had recently made to marry Lennie. It was a choice that would forever alter the public's perception of her and further estrange her from her black middle-class roots. For years, she had been a role model—an undeniable symbol of black achievement—and would not allow herself to make a false step while in the public eye. But by marrying a man

Horne in a performance at New York City's Paramount Theater in 1947. Her voice, according to music critic John S. Wilson of the New York Times, is "with range and color and control that are rare in top singers."

who was white, she would be jeopardizing her entire image. Interracial marriage was not well regarded by many of the nation's blacks or whites. In fact, in some places, including California, it was against the law.

Deciding that it was best to marry while they were away from the public spotlight, Horne and Hayton set sail for Europe in October 1947. Lena, who had booked engagements in London and Paris, was determined to marry Lennie overseas, in secret. She figured that by the time they returned to the United States, people might be ready to accept them as a couple.

What she did not count on was that they would be returning to the United States in time for another kind of ostracism. ◀❂▶

7
THE
CHANGING
SCENE

LENA HORNE WAS welcomed in London with open arms. Her appearance at the London Casino, a small cabaret in the city's theater district, in late 1947 made her one of the first black American stars to perform in England since the start of World War II. Sailors in the Royal Navy remembered her from the Hollywood movies that had been screened for them during wartime. Devoted music fans knew her from her Charlie Barnet and Artie Shaw recordings from the early 1940s.

After conquering the London audiences, Horne crossed the English Channel with Hayton and journeyed to Paris. There her two-week engagement at the Club Champs-Élysées was also met with thunderous applause. One French newspaper even featured her picture on its front page above the caption *Un Triomphe*.

When her tour ended, Lena and Lennie were married in a quiet ceremony in the City of Lights. Again she wore a black wedding dress—this time a stunning, highly fashionable Balenciaga—and carried a bouquet of violets that Lennie had bought from a street vendor. They exchanged plain gold wedding bands and then celebrated the day's events with a few friends at a small café overlooking the Seine.

In Europe, the newlyweds encountered few racial problems. But this sense of calm quickly disappeared

Cast as the first glamorous black star in America, Horne discovered that she had been turned into a positive role model who was constantly scrutinized by the public.

once they headed back to the United States. The couple sailed home on the SS *America*, only to learn that the ship's black workers had been denied entry into a labor union. Lena, in an act of solidarity with the crewmen, refused to perform at the captain's gala because he branded the blacks as mischief makers.

Horne arrived in New York City on December 22, 1947, and immediately plunged into a hectic schedule. She commuted regularly between New York, where Gail attended school, and California, where her husband worked. Lennie's contract with MGM called for him to remain with the studio until 1953 (Lena's contract with the studio would end in 1950 with the making of *The Duchess of Idaho*).

Always on the go, Horne found the late 1940s to be a very difficult period in her life. "Unfortunately," she said in her autobiography, "I could neither slow down my work schedule nor find a job that allowed

While in Europe in 1947, Horne took time away from her professional engagements to speak out on civil rights. She is shown here preparing to address a student gathering in London.

me to stay put in one location for any length of time." When she had some free time, she usually had to choose between seeing her daughter on the East Coast and spending time with her husband out west.

What made life even more difficult for Horne was that she and Lennie insisted on keeping their marriage a secret from the public. They wanted to avoid intense scrutiny into their lives by the media, and they did not want to stir up any misguided anger by their fans. They did inform their relatives, however, but with the expected results: Most of Lena's family, including her father, immediately stopped talking to her. The estrangement between Teddy and Lena, which lasted for several years, foreshadowed the rough times that were to come for her.

In 1948, Horne went to Hollywood to appear in *Words and Music*, a film biography of the songwriting team of Richard Rodgers and Lorenz Hart. With Lennie serving as the movie's music director, the newlyweds got to see each other fairly often while the film was being shot. Nevertheless, Lena spent most of the year away from him, on the cabaret circuit. Her solo act prompted *Life* magazine to dub her "the season's top nightclub attraction" for 1948, but she took little pleasure in such accolades. She was extremely unhappy to be on the road, away from her family for extended periods of time. "Gradually," she said, "without being aware of it, a kind of despair began to creep over me."

Horne managed to hide her feelings from the public. Onstage and at political functions, she continued to show her usual zeal, especially when these two interests merged. Such was the case in January 1949, when Harry S. Truman asked her to sing at his inaugural ball in Washington, D.C. The president had invited her to perform at the celebrity-studded affair as a way of thanking the 31-year-old entertainer for her support during the recent presidential election.

Lena with her second husband, Lennie Hayton.

Lena had publicly backed Truman in 1948 after he created the Fair Employment Board to eliminate discrimination in government agencies and issued an executive order to desegregate the army.

A number of people on the political scene, however, were hardly so gracious. A dark political storm had been brewing in the nation for some time, and it was about to erupt. When it did, the civil liberties of many Americans, including Horne, were undermined for a number of years.

The trouble first began in 1938, when the House of Representatives established the House Un-American Activities Committee (HUAC) to investigate the affairs of U.S. citizens whom the government suspected of acting against the interests of their country. The committee was originally formed to put a stop to communist propaganda, but it soon managed to do more than that. By the 1940s, many prominent (and, most often, liberal-minded) individuals thought to be dangerous to the welfare of the United States had been brought before the committee to testify about their political beliefs.

Nine years later, this feverish witch-hunt, expanded because of America's postwar fear of communism and the rise of the Soviet Union as an international power, took hold of the entertainment industry. A group of powerful television executives, seeking to protect their own interests in what was a new and growing medium, announced they would never "knowingly" employ the services of people who belonged to the Communist party or other "subversive" organizations. Claiming that their actions were for the good of America, they put together a roster of people—prominent writers, producers, and directors—whose politics they regarded as questionable and subsequently banned them from all television work. Blacklisting, a form of discrimination that not only prevented people from finding work but tarnished their professional reputation in the process, had begun.

In 1950, Senator Joseph McCarthy began a relentless campaign against the alleged "Red Menace," and others were quick to follow. The powerful resources of media magnate William Randolph Hearst responded by whipping the nation into a frenzy of red-baiting as popular columnists, including Walter Winchell, Hedda Hopper, and George Sokolsky, suggested new suspects and cleared old ones daily. Individuals were dishonored, careers were destroyed, and several people were even imprisoned over the next few years, until this method of slander was declared illegal.

In June 1950, Horne was listed as a communist sympathizer in *Red Channels* and *Counterattack*, two magazines distributed to radio and television stations throughout America. A major reason for her being singled out was her friendship with Paul Robeson, who was noted for speaking out in support of blacks and the working class. Her work on the Council on African Affairs and her support of the liberal Hollywood Independent Citizens Committee of the Arts, Sciences, and Professions, for whom she did countless benefit performances, also made her a ready target.

Horne was never officially named as a communist, so she did not have to testify before any congressional committees. But in many circles, being listed was tantamount to being guilty, and her professional life was adversely affected. No one in the burgeoning television industry would hire her.

Fortunately for Horne, the nightclub circuit paid little attention to the actions of blacklisters. By 1952, she was earning as much as $12,500 a week for performing at the Sands Hotel in Las Vegas and at other top night spots. Yet she continued to be troubled by the course of her professional life. To work as a singer in America, she said, "seemed to me just one big

During the 1950s, Senator Joseph McCarthy presided over a series of highly publicized hearings to investigate supposedly subversive Americans. Because of her friendship with communist sympathizer Paul Robeson, who was among the targets of these hearings, Horne was temporarily banned from making any television appearances.

night club, a weary succession of similar cities, one nasty little fight after another over some aspect of racial segregation, a series of questioning glances directed at me and my husband." By this time, Lena and Lennie Hayton had announced their marriage to the public—and had gotten bombarded with hate mail as a result.

In 1953, with Gail happily ensconced at a Quaker boarding school in upstate New York, Lena sold both of her houses and spent the next few years moving with her husband from one hotel suite to another, in a seemingly endless rhythm of life on the road. They traveled from Las Vegas and Monte Carlo to Scotland and Israel, and Lena was celebrated everywhere they went as a glamorous star clothed in the latest designer fashions. Rumor had it that she never wore the same gown twice.

Except for performing in clubs, there was little else for Horne to do. In 1955, she returned briefly to Hollywood to film a musical segment, arranged and conducted by Lennie, for the movie *Meet Me in Las Vegas*. But no other film roles came her way. She had risen as high in the film industry as the white studio

Horne was one of the biggest draws in Las Vegas even though she rarely enjoyed performing there. The popular resort center provided her with steady work, however.

executives allowed her to go. As was usually the case, Hollywood felt that black stars were not in vogue.

Instead of going back on the road, Horne decided to return to New York. The city, long regarded as the capital of the theater, had recently become the center of the television industry, and she was looking for new challenges. In 1956, she and Lennie took an apartment on Manhattan's Upper West Side.

Much as she had done a decade earlier when she wanted to take on more work, Horne arranged an informal meeting with a man of authority. In 1945, she had met with studio head Louis B. Mayer; this time, she arranged an interview with George Sokolsky, the political columnist who held enormous sway within the ranks of blacklisters, in an effort to open up job opportunities for herself in television and radio.

Horne, in mid-career, was usually backed by an orchestra led by Lennie Hayton (center). She was also assisted by the hard-working Ralph Harris, who became her manager at Lennie's suggestion.

The meeting went smoothly—Lena listened quietly while the journalist lectured her on her political waywardness—and within days she saw her name removed from the blacklist in *Red Channels* and *Counterattack*. Shortly thereafter, she was booked on two of the nation's most popular television shows: "The Ed Sullivan Show" and "The Tonight Show" starring Steve Allen.

In 1956, Horne also resumed making records. She had not cut a record in five years because she believed that her voice was not well suited to the medium. RCA Victor was willing to take a chance with her, however, and the sales of her album proved the com-

Horne recording for RCA Victor in New York. Her 1957 album Lena Horne at the Waldorf-Astoria, *cut after a five-year absence from the studio, marked a highly successful return to making records.*

pany to be right. *Lena Horne at the Waldorf-Astoria*, released in 1957, became the largest-selling album by a female performer in RCA's history.

That same year, Horne stretched herself artistically in yet another way: She accepted the female lead in the Broadway-bound musical *Jamaica*. The show was originally written for calypso king Harry Belafonte, but it was ultimately cast with actor Ricardo Montalban as the male lead. Horne took on the role of the earthy Savanna.

During the early stages of rehearsal, the play had all the earmarks of a total disaster: The producer fought with the lyricist, the director tried to please too many people and ended up pleasing none, and the advance reviews of the show were so bad that the cast members stopped reading them. Yet none of these problems seemed to deter the theatergoing public. Thanks to Horne's star power, the show had a huge advance sale.

As Horne continued to prepare for her first Broadway opening in more than 20 years, she could not help but feel that the success of the show rested on the strength of her performance, because she was the box-office draw. At times, she wondered how strong her performance would be. It seemed as though she had forgotten everything she knew about performing in a play. "I had worshiped at the shrine of the theater from the lowly depths of cabarets for so long that I was in shock when I walked out on a stage," she said.

On opening night, director Bobby Lewis told Horne to make her entrance onto the stage just like she belonged there. At first, she did not know exactly what he meant. It was only when a huge bouquet of flowers arrived in her dressing room with a card bearing the inscription *Savanna, we love you, The Crew* that she understood. She was a hometown favorite awaited by her adoring fans. She had no reason to worry about how she would be received.

Away from the public spotlight, a not-so-reserved Horne dances at a house party.

Acting with supreme confidence, Horne won over the theater critics—the *New York Post* cited "her enormous and stirring skill at projecting a song for everything that is in it"—and the show did as well. *Jamaica* became the hit of the Broadway season. It ran for 555 performances and did not close until the spring of 1959.

The grind of performing in a Broadway show can call for an actress to appear in as many as nine performances a week, including five shows each weekend. It is a work load that can wear down even the most dedicated performer. But appearing in *Jamaica* did not faze Horne. The grueling schedule only served to energize her.

During the run of *Jamaica*, Horne was elected an honorary member of Delta Sigma Theta, an influential women's service organization composed of black college graduates. Opting to take part in an effective service organization rather than lobby for civil rights on her own, she participated actively in voter registration drives and job training programs for young women. Through her work with the sorority, she also revived her ties with the National Council of Negro Women, founded by Frank Horne's fellow black-cabinet member Mary McLeod Bethune, who had also been a close friend of Cora Horne's.

As Lena became more and more involved in the everyday problems of black America, it became apparent to her how removed she was from the lives of her fellow blacks. Ever since she had entered show business, she had been a product of what she called "the white man's world." The entertainment industry was owned and operated by whites who had given her the opportunity to become a shining star but had prevented her from ranging wherever she wanted. "I never liked the role," she said, "but I had gone with it." The times had called for her to be a symbol—to blacks, a model of achievement, and to whites, an exemplar of respectability—and she had complied.

But now the times had changed. A new generation of blacks, led by the Reverend Martin Luther King, Jr., and other black activists, was no longer satisfied with white tokenism. Instead of being allowed only a few symbols of black success, they insisted on gaining their full civil rights.

When Horne took a close look at these changes, she realized what had taken place. "I was an alien in the world of the average Negro," she said. ✺

SHOW

THE
MAGAZINE
OF
THE
ARTS

75 CENTS
SEPTEMBER 19

**BREAKING
THE WHITE
BARRIER:
LENA HORNE
SPEAKS
ON THE ARTIST
AND THE
NEGRO REVOLT**

8

ACT TWO

ON THE NIGHT of February 17, 1960—one year after *Jamaica* closed—another, much more militant side of Lena Horne was presented to the world at large. She was in Los Angeles with her husband, waiting for Kay Thompson, an old friend from their MGM days, to arrive for a dinner date at the Luau Restaurant in Beverly Hills. When Thompson failed to show up, Lennie left the table to telephone her.

Meanwhile, a drunken diner near Horne began to demand service from a waiter who was carrying a tray of drinks to Lena's table. "I'll be with you shortly," the waiter told the inebriated man, "as soon as I serve Lena Horne." Displeased by this delay, the customer let loose with a racial slur before yelling, "Where is Lena Horne, anyway?" Horne, taking in the entire scene, stood up and hurled an ashtray, a table lamp, and several glasses at the drunk, all the while screaming furiously at him, "Here I am, you bastard, I'm the nigger you couldn't see."

The bigoted, slightly bloodied man was ejected from the restaurant, and Horne was celebrated by the media for her willingness to fight back at him. Letters from sympathetic blacks who identified with her sense of outrage poured in from around the country. She had touched the hearts and minds of the very people from whom she felt separated.

The incident and its aftermath confirmed for Horne that she had the respect of her peers and need not think of herself solely as a symbolic figure in the civil rights movement. Further proof of her importance to

The September 1963 issue of Show *magazine featured Horne on its cover, symbolically hidden by a white barrier. She wrote in the accompanying article, entitled "I Just Want to Be Myself": "I don't want to sing the same old songs or act in the same stereotyped musicals. . . . I think that songs can be written and plays and musicals produced which simply put the Negro in the context of the world."*

the struggle for black rights occurred in the spring of 1963, a time when racial tensions in the United States were approaching the breaking point. The sweeping changes called for by civil rights marchers in the 1950s had failed to materialize, and massive nation-wide protests were being threatened by Martin Luther King, Jr.

In May 1963, Horne received a phone call at her recently purchased home in Palm Springs, California, from author James Baldwin. He wanted her to join a small group, made up mostly of prominent blacks—including Harry Belafonte, playwright Lorraine Hansberry, and psychologist Kenneth Clark—to discuss the mounting racial crisis. U.S. attorney general Robert Kennedy had asked Baldwin to arrange the meeting, which the nation's chief legal counsel called a gathering of "the Negroes other Negroes listen to." It was to be held at his residence in New York, and the topics Kennedy wanted to discuss were to include segregation and racial violence in the South. At first, Horne balked at attending. "I had begun to convince myself that all of us 'firsts'—first glamour girl, first baseball player, first this-that-and-the-other—had

By the spring of 1963, the non-violent civil rights movement led by the Reverend Martin Luther King, Jr. (seated at left of table), had begun to encounter violent resistance in Birmingham, Alabama. "I was in agony," Horne said of the situation, "and also feeling completely impotent to do anything."

reached the end of our usefulness," she said. But her husband helped convince her to make the trip, and she flew to New York for the meeting.

Little came out of the conference. Kennedy stressed that great strides were being made in racial relations, and the black leaders in the room emphasized that much more needed to be done. Then, Jerome Smith, a field-worker for a prominent activist group, the Student Nonviolent Coordinating Committee (SNCC), began to speak. He told the assembly that no one could really understand the explosive situation in the South unless they lived there. He recounted the injustices that had been heaped upon him, the beatings that had left him permanently disabled, and finished by stating unequivocally that he could no longer tolerate the way blacks were treated in the South.

Smith's testimony severely shook everyone at the meeting. Although he was still a young man, his weariness and bitterness deeply moved his listeners. His speech was a call for action, and after the meeting adjourned, Horne contacted the NAACP and told the organization she wanted to work in the South on its behalf.

The following month, Horne, accompanied by Billy Strayhorn, appeared at a voter registration rally in Jackson, Mississippi. The rally had been organized by Medgar Evers, who headed the Mississippi branch of the NAACP. This was a highly visible position that often placed him in danger. His house had recently been firebombed, and he had been told by NAACP officials to keep off the streets for fear of his safety.

Horne boosted everyone's spirits at the rally by singing "This Little Light of Mine," and her own spirits lifted when she saw the work that Evers was accomplishing. In the short time Lena was in Jackson, she learned to marvel at his superhuman energy, strong

The widow of Medgar Evers and her two children view the body of the slain civil-rights leader on June 14, 1963. He was gunned down in Jackson, Mississippi, several days after Horne attended an NAACP-sponsored rally with him.

spiritual faith, and personal warmth. A day after she returned to New York, she was stunned to hear that he had been gunned down outside his Mississippi home by white racists. A double-barreled shotgun had blasted him in the back.

Within months of Evers's murder, civil rights leaders A. Philip Randolph and his longtime associate Bayard Rustin coordinated a rally they called the March for Jobs and Freedom: a civil rights march through the nation's capital that would direct the attention of U.S. citizens to the plight of their black countrymen. Security for the rally, held on August 28, 1963, was very tight. President John F. Kennedy was extremely worried that the demonstration might turn violent.

Yet the marchers, although emotionally stirred by the day's events, proved to be quite peaceful. More than 250,000 protesters made the symbolic walk from the Washington Monument to the Lincoln Memorial in a show of unity and brotherhood. Horne was there with her friends and family to hear Randolph begin the rally by telling the crowd, "Let the nation and the world know the meaning of our numbers," and to hear Martin Luther King, Jr., conclude the activities by offering his grand vision of a just society. "I have a dream today," he told the demonstrators in his haunting address.

For the rest of the decade, Horne spent the bulk of her time participating in rallies and roundtable discussions to further the rights of black Americans. Her club performances reflected these concerns as she added protest songs to her repertoire. At one benefit, she performed a protest piece entitled "Now!"; the lyrics were penned by songwriters Betty Comden and Adolph Green and were performed to the tune of an old Jewish favorite, "Hava Nagillah." Horne's recorded version of this civil rights song caused such a sensation that a number of radio stations refused to play it.

In 1969, Horne appeared in her first American television special, "Lena in Concert." She also returned briefly to Hollywood and filmed *Death of a Gunfighter* with actor Richard Widmark. The movie was her first attempt at a straight dramatic role. As usual, she received excellent reviews. The movie was a box-office failure, however.

Greater sorrows soon followed. In 1971, Lena's father died from emphysema. Five months later, her son, who had been suffering from a rare kidney disease, also died. Then her husband died. Within less than a year, she had to endure the deaths of the three most important men in her life.

"I suddenly ground to a halt," Horne recalled one year later. "I couldn't do anything." Devastated, she decided to retire to her home in Santa Barbara, California.

Lena's son, Teddy.

In 1972, Horne resumed touring. Working with Count Basie, singer Vic Damone, comedian Alan King, and others, she performed in theaters and clubs throughout the United States and Europe. The following year, she teamed up with singer Tony Bennett and went on an international tour that they launched with a television special entitled "Tony and Lena." The American leg of their tour began in the fall of 1974, with three weeks of sold-out performances at the Minskoff Theater in New York. Then they took their act across the country, topping off the tour with a smash-hit engagement at the Shubert Theater in Los Angeles.

Afterward, Horne returned to New York so she could take care of her long-estranged mother. The strains in their difficult and complicated relationship were somewhat eased by the time Edna died in early 1977. Lena's instinctive reaction to her mother's death was to draw closer than ever to her recently married daughter, Gail, and her two young granddaughters, Amy and Jenny. By this time, Lena had cut back on her touring and was performing about 20 weeks each year.

Horne performs a musical number with singers Dean Martin and the Andrew Sisters on a television variety program. For more than 15 years, she sought her own television show but was unable to find anyone willing to produce a show starring a black performer.

In August 1977, Horne made another movie: the film version of the hit Broadway musical *The Wiz*. Based on L. Frank Baum's classic of children's literature, *The Wonderful Wizard of Oz*, the film starred singers Diana Ross as Dorothy and Michael Jackson as the Scarecrow and comedian Richard Pryor as the title character. Lena was cast as Glinda, the Good Witch of the North, and poured her heart into the rousing song "Believe in Yourself." There was, as one critic noted, "an intensity, sometimes warm and intimate, sometimes ominously commanding, in every syllable she projects."

As Horne neared her sixtieth birthday, she contemplated retiring from show business. But she could not make herself do it. In May 1980, after receiving four standing ovations at a benefit for the Duke Ellington School of Arts held at the Kennedy Center in Washington, D.C., she commented, "I always say I'm going to stop performing, but then I get an audience like the one tonight and I get all corny again."

Lena flanked by her granddaughters Jenny (far left) and Amy (right) and her daughter, Gail, after the opening of her one-woman show in 1981.

Nothing, however, could have prepared Horne for the reception of the one-woman limited engagement that she unveiled at Broadway's Nederlander Theater on March 12, 1981. *Lena Horne: The Lady and Her Music* took the entertainment world by storm. Backed by a powerful orchestra and three singer-dancers, her show was a triumphant retrospective of her career. Through musical sequences, it followed her growth as a singer—from her early days at the Cotton Club to her MGM years to her celebrated status as a vivacious nightclub entertainer. She performed many of the songs that had become identified with her, including "Surrey with the Fringe on the Top," "Can't Help Lovin' Dat Man," "Love Me or Leave Me," "Bewitched, Bothered, and Bewildered," and "Life Goes On."

Horne's retrospective show, Lena Horne: The Lady and Her Music, *"had the sort of effect that only the greatest theatrical events have," according to* Newsweek *magazine. It ultimately ran longer than any other one-person show on Broadway.*

Horne and her daughter, author Gail Lumet Buckley, with two of the many awards they have garnered. Buckley's book on the life and times of her family, The Hornes, was honored as "a special chronicle of the American scene."

Lena Horne: The Lady and Her Music was a musical tour de force that left audiences elated and critics stunned by her talent. It also left no doubt that Horne was much more than a symbol: She was a national treasure. The limited engagement was extended again and again, and it eventually became the longest-running one-person show in the history of Broadway.

Horne's exceptional performance in her one-woman show earned her the entertainment industry's top awards, including the Antoinette Perry (Tony) Award, the Drama Desk Award, the Handel Medallion, the Actors Equity Paul Robeson Award, the Dance Theatre of Harlem's Emergence Award, and two Grammy Awards for the original cast album. In addition to

Horne during a performance of her landmark one-woman show.

these honors, she also received the Spingarn Medal, the highest award given by the NAACP, and the Kennedy Center Honors for a lifetime of achievement in the performing arts. Her portrait now hangs in the National Portrait Gallery in Washington, D.C.

Lena Horne: The Lady and Her Music closed in New York on Horne's sixty-fifth birthday. She then took the show on the road, electrifying audiences across the country and in Europe. After she ended her international tour, she returned to the United

States and, in 1985, moved from the West Coast to Washington, D.C., so she could be close to her daughter and granddaughters.

Horne's professional appearances have become less frequent since she stopped touring with *Lena Horne: The Lady and Her Music*. Yet it is unlikely that anyone who has ever watched her perform can forget her powerful stage presence. All one has to do is recall Lena in her one-woman show, the highlight of which was undoubtedly her rendition of "Stormy Weather."

When the show was in its rehearsal stages, Horne was not sure that she should perform the song. After all, she had sung "Stormy Weather" at almost every concert she had ever given. When the director of the show insisted that her fans would want to hear it, the song was put back in. Then it was dropped once more. As it turned out, the song was removed from the show and reinserted so many times during rehearsals that it became a running joke among the entire company.

Finally, Horne hit upon the idea of performing "Stormy Weather" twice in the show. The first time, early on in the act, she performed the song in a simple, straightforward manner, just as she had done during her early days in Hollywood, when she was still a maturing singer. Then, in act two, she sang "Stormy Weather" again, but as she had never sung it before: with a depth and resonance that comes only after years of experience.

With this one song, Horne sought to emphasize her evolution as a singer and sum up her personal life. Each time the final strains of "Stormy Weather" faded softly into silence, she stood alone on the stage, bathed in a circle of light. This theatrical coup stunned the crowd. Then, just like those who watched her Cotton Club audition more than a half century earlier, they rose to their feet, roaring wildly with appreciation and applauding for Lena Horne. ❧

APPENDIX

SELECTED DISCOGRAPHY

The recordings that Lena Horne has made during her career as a solo performer have been issued by a number of record companies. The following albums are all currently available and should serve as a good introduction to her music.

Give the Lady What She Wants (RCA Records)

Jazz Master (DRG Records)

The Lady (Dunhill Compact Classics)

Lena (RCA Records)

Lena Goes Latin (DRG Records)

Live on Broadway (Qwest Records)

Live in Hollywood (Liberty Records)

Lovely and Alive (RCA Records)

The Men in My Life (Three Cherry Records)

One and Only (Polydor Records)

20 Golden Pieces of Lena Horne (Bulldog Records)

CHRONOLOGY

————— ❦ —————

1917   Born Lena Mary Calhoun Horne in Brooklyn, New York, on June 30

1933   Becomes a chorus girl at the Cotton Club in Harlem

1934   Appears in first Broadway show, *Dance with Your Gods*

1935   Joins Noble Sissle's Society Orchestra

1937   Marries Louis Jones; daughter, Gail, is born

1938   Appears in first Hollywood film, *The Duke Is Tops*

1940   Joins Charlie Barnet's band; son, Teddy, is born

1941   Launches solo career at Café Society in New York; records first album

1942   Appears in *Panama Hattie*

1943   Appears in *Thousands Cheer, Cabin in the Sky, Stormy Weather, I Dood It!,* and *Swing Fever*

1944   Appears in *Broadway Rhythm* and *Two Girls and a Sailor*; divorces Louis Jones

1946   Appears in *Ziegfeld Follies* and *Till the Clouds Roll By*

1947   Marries Lennie Hayton

1946   Appears in *Words and Music*

1950   Appears in *The Duchess of Idaho*

1956   Appears in *Meet Me in Las Vegas*

1957   Stars on Broadway in *Jamaica*; records *Lena Horne at the Waldorf-Astoria*

1969   Appears in first television special, "Lena in Concert," and in *Death of a Gunfighter*

1977   Appears in *The Wiz*

1981   *Lena Horne: The Lady and Her Music* opens on Broadway

1982   Awarded the Spingarn Medal

FURTHER READING

Arstein, Helen, ed. *In Person: Lena Horne.* New York: Greenberg, 1950.

Buckley, Gail Lumet. *The Hornes: An American Family.* New York: Knopf, 1986.

Charters, Samuel, and Leonard Kunstadt. *Jazz: A History of the New York Scene.* 1962. Reprint. New York: Da Capo Press, 1982.

Dorbin, Arnold. *Voices of Joy, Voices of Freedom.* New York: Coward-McCann, 1972.

Fox, Ted. *Showtime at the Apollo.* New York: Holt, Rinehart & Winston, 1983.

Gourse, Leslie. *Louis' Children: American Jazz Singers.* New York: Morrow, 1984.

Haskins, James. *The Cotton Club.* New York: Random House, 1977.

———. *Lena.* New York: Stein and Day, 1984.

———. *Lena Horne.* New York: Coward-McCann, 1983.

Horne, Lena, and Richard Schickel. *Lena.* New York: Doubleday, 1965.

INDEX

ACKNOWLEDGMENTS

We gratefully thank Gail Lumet Buckley for providing many of the photographs that appear in this work.

PICTURE CREDITS

AP/Wide World Photos: pp. 66, 89, 100, 103, 105, 118, 119, 120; Bethune Museum and Archive: pp. 67, 90, 93; The Bettmann Archive: pp. 10, 12; Brooklyn Historical Society: pp. 33, 34; Gail Lumet Buckley: pp. 15, 18, 21, 24, 25, 28, 29, 30, 31, 32, 35, 36, 43, 50, 60, 88, 94, 95, 104, 110, 115; Jerry Cooke/*Life* magazine: p. 108; Culver Photos: pp. 56, 57, 70, 72, 77, 81, 86; Frank Driggs Collection: pp. 26, 38, 40, 48, 52, 54, 64, 65, 78, 84, 96, 97, 98, 106, 116; William Gottlieb: p. 91; Collection of Edouard Plummer: p. 92; Duncan Scheidt: p. 16; Schomburg Center for Research of Black Culture, New York Public Library: pp. 14, 45, 51, 69, 74, 82, 101; UPI/Bettmann Newsphotos: pp. 68, 112, 114, 117; Carl Van Vechten Collection/ Yale University Library: p. 41; Yale University Library: p. 62

LESLIE PALMER holds a degree in theater and literature from Sarah Lawrence College. She has worked as a writer and editor for several publishing houses in New York City and currently works for a major magazine company.

NATHAN IRVIN HUGGINS is W.E.B. Du Bois Professor of History and Director of the W.E.B. Du Bois Institute for Afro-American Research at Harvard University. He previously taught at Columbia University. Professor Huggins is the author of numerous books, including *Black Odyssey: The Afro-American Ordeal in Slavery*, *The Harlem Renaissance*, and *Slave and Citizen: The Life of Frederick Douglass*.